YOUR INNER YOU

LESLIE B. FLYNN

While this book is designed for your personal profit and enjoyment, it is also intended for group study. A Leader's Guide with Victor Multiuse Transparency Masters is available from your local bookstore or from the publisher.

VICTOR BOOKS a division of SP Publications, Inc.

WHEATON. ILLINOIS 60187

Offices also in
Whitby. Ontario. Canada
Amersham-on-the-Hill. Bucks. England

Recommended Dewey Decimal Classification: 248
Suggested Subject Heading: SPIRITUAL LIFE

Library of Congress Catalog Card Number: 84-50141
ISBN: 0-89693-378-4

© 1984 by SP Publications, Inc. All rights reserved
Printed in the United States of America

VICTOR BOOKS
A division of SP Publications, Inc.
Wheaton, Illinois 60187

Contents

To our friends
and advisors of many years,
Stuart and Jewel Gray

1

The Inner Sanctum

An exile in Chaldea in 600 B.C., the Prophet Ezekiel was shown what was happening in Jerusalem hundreds of miles to the west. In a vision from God he was carried to the door of the temple court and then behind a hole in the wall to a secret door of an inner sanctum. Entering, he saw on a wall a host of heathen gods in the forms of abominable creeping things.

The elders of Israel were practicing idolatry in a private chamber, unknown to the outside world. Safely concealed in the seclusion of a supposedly holy place, they revelled in their idolatrous orgies. Later, they would appear on the streets as respectable citizens. All the time they were saying, "The Lord does not see us."

This passage of Scripture, Ezekiel 8:5-12, suggests that every person has his own inner sanctum. Ezekiel spoke of what these ancients were doing "in the dark, every man in the chambers of his imagery" (v. 12). The RSV puts it, "every man in his room of pictures."

The Mind

A young New York street kid offered to sell a very expensive watch to a stranger for only $5. "Why so cheap?" asked the man. The boy replied, "It's got no insides."

You and I aren't made that way. Although we are body, we are more than that. We possess an immaterial part that includes soul, spirit, and mind. God's image in us is both intellectual and moral. We have the capacity for both reason and righteousness. In fact, thinking is probably our foremost activity. Our ability to reason makes us superior to the animal world. We can think discursively and go through the process of a syllogism. We have been given the physical apparatus to express our thoughts through involved linguistic sounds called speech. Because of our minds, we are able to invent, enjoy aesthetics, and appreciate humor—feats all beyond nonintellectual creatures. Descartes said, "I think, therefore I am." John Owen, vice-chancellor of Oxford University, stated, "The mind is the leading faculty of the soul." A little girl, asked what her soul was, replied, "My soul is my think."

Thinking is man's main occupation. We think all the time, even when we sleep. Sleep experts tell us that a parade of mental images passes before our inward vision much of the night, and that this process helps our mental health. Some people discover solutions during sleep to problems that were on their minds before bedtime. Though we can stop entertaining certain thoughts in our minds, we cannot stop the activity of thinking, whether our eyes are open or closed. We may retreat from the outside world with its bombardment of stimuli into our own little world, but it will be a world of thought.

A husband and wife were sitting at the breakfast table on his day off. She said to him, "Please don't think of playing golf this morning." He replied, "It's the farthest thing from my mind. Please pass the putter."

The Heart

The Bible speaks of man's inner self as "heart," which often indicates the person himself, the center of moral, spiritual, and intellectual life, the source of vital action. John Owen said:

> The heart in Scripture is variously used, sometimes for the mind and understanding, sometimes for the will, sometimes for the affections, sometimes for the conscience, sometimes for the whole soul. Generally, it denotes the whole soul of man and all the faculties of it, not absolutely, but as they are all one principle of moral operation, as they all concur in our doing of good and evil (ISBE, vol. II, p. 1351, article on *Heart*).

The heart of man is his worst part before regeneration and his finest part afterward. The biggest problem before conversion is to win the heart *to* God; the major difficulty after conversion is to keep the heart *with* God. Paul calls the heart the "inner man" (Eph. 3:16). Significantly, in the biblical commands to love God, the heart always takes precedence. When we love God with all our heart, this includes mind and soul (Deut. 6:5; Matt. 22:37).

It is this inner self that God searches with His high intensity lights. When the Prophet Samuel thought that Jesse's handsome eldest son would certainly be God's choice to succeed Saul as king of Israel, the Lord replied, "Man looks at the outward appearance, but the Lord looks at the heart" (1 Sam. 16:7, NASB).

Jesus pointed out to the Pharisees their preoccupation with ceremonial, exterior cleansing, while neglecting the condition of their insides (Luke 11:39). He likened them to sepulchres which, though whitewashed outside, were full of dead men's bones within (Matt. 23:27). He also warned, "That which is highly esteemed among men is detestable in the sight of God" (Luke 16:15, NASB).

Peter insisted that our adorning be not outward in nature, but rather "the hidden person of the heart, . . . a gentle and quiet spirit, which is precious in the sight of God" (1 Peter 3:3-4, NASB). At the Transfiguration, God revealed the inner self of His Son in all the brilliant splendor of His glory.

When God is described as no respecter of persons, the word means literally "face-receiver." God is not a face-receiver but He is a heart-regarder. In the final analysis, we are what we think in the solitude of our souls.

Fallen Human Nature

Because of the Fall, man has lost his original righteousness. His inner, moral nature is corrupt. Every person born into our world possesses a bent toward evil, which is early displayed in childhood and which remains throughout life. This depravity extends to every part of human nature including the mind, which has become blinded, darkened, unable to receive the things of the Spirit, and antagonistic toward God (Rom. 8:7; 1 Cor. 2:14; 2 Cor. 4:4; Eph. 4:18).

Because our moral brakes do not match our mental horsepower, all our vaunted scientific advances cannot rescue us from our moral morass. We learned to build planes, then turned them into bombers. We unleashed atomic energy, only to manufacture nuclear warheads. We invented TV, but degraded it with violence and sex. We have the means to master the earth but cannot control ourselves. A person can possess mental excellence and also be morally corrupt. Candidates for Ph.D. degrees have been caught stealing books needed for research from public libraries. A young woman with an MBA deliberately soiled a dress so she could buy it at a reduced price. Medical students have been known to use razors with surgical preciseness to cut valuable paragraphs from rare scientific journals.

Because of its inborn sinfulness, the inner sanctum has the capacity of becoming a chamber of horrors. The following adjectives, all used in the Bible to describe the heart, show the radical corruption of the inner man: hardened (Ex. 4:21), godless (Job 36:13), perverse (Prov. 11:20), wicked (Prov. 26:23), deceitful and desperately sick (Jer. 17:9), and depraved (Rom. 1:28). Jesus declared that man's inner sanctuary is the source of his wickedness.

> For from within, out of the heart of men, proceed evil thoughts and fornications, thefts, murders, adulteries, deeds of covetousing and wickedness, as well as deceit, sensuality, envy, slander, pride, and foolishness. All these evil things proceed from within, and defile the man (Mark 7:21-23, NASB).

• Sexual impurity. The Bible speaks of man's heart as "evil from his youth" (Gen. 8:21, NASB), also as "having eyes full of adultery and that never cease from sin" (2 Peter 2:14, NASB). By the millions, people eat out of the garbage can of modern trash. Reading material depicting the Playboy philosophy tends to make their minds septic tanks. We should take care about the pictures we let decorate the walls of our chamber of imagery.

• Malice. In many colleges and high schools, William Golding's *Lord of the Flies* is required reading. The story concerns boys who survive atomic war, struggle to reestablish civilized moral and social order, but who tragically revert to savagery. On a primitive island, under pressure of their basic needs, refinements fall away, releasing the dark, tangled jungle of human personality. The boys slide into blood-lust, mutilation, and even murder.

A few years ago, a young man teetered on the ninth floor of a Boston hotel ledge for hours, threatening to leap. For an hour and one-half, the voices from the street below kept shouting, "Jump!" Finally, he was coaxed inside. A navy commander with three rows of campaign ribbons, referring to the sadistic taunts of the crowd, said quietly, "In two wars I've never seen anything so terrible."

Man's inhumanity to man is proverbial. Unbelievable methods of torture have been devised through the centuries. I heard of someone who recently stripped a man naked, smeared him with honey, then hung him helplessly over a beehive.

Six weeks after the Tylenol deaths in the fall of 1983, after winnowing through thousands of leads, interviews, and case reports, the attorney general of Illinois said that out there are a lot of people "who are incredibly hateful, who have contempt for their fellowman, who show it in various ways" (*New York Times,* 11/9/83).

• Deceit. How prevalent is the habit of falsifying the truth! We tell straight lies with a poker face, or half lies like Abraham did, when he said Sarah was his sister. We use proper words in a misleading sense, or speak with mental reservation, like saying someone is out, when we mean he is just out to that particular caller. Or we act the lie by a shrug of the shoulder, intonation of voice, glance of the eye, or emphasis on a portion of a sentence. We can lie through false affection, as Judas did. Or we can misquote, handle the facts carelessly, or exaggerate.

Rationalization, a term which reminds us of our God-given rational ability, refers to a mishandling of this wonderful power, so as to excuse wrong conduct. Such misuse of reason might lead a poor lady, finding a purse on a church pew, to exclaim, "Here's my answer to prayer!"

• Covetousness. The above vices, though commencing in the inner sanctum, result in overt, public misbehavior. But many sins can be committed within the heart and remain private, unseen by others. Covetousness, the excessive desire for what one has not, especially for what belongs to another, can be done in church, undetected by human eye.

Many an executive hides deep-seated ambition for higher salary and greater power. Proverbs says, "The eyes of man are never satisfied" (27:20).

• Resentment. When a lady's blood pressure registered extremely high, she explained to the doctor, "I just had a heated argument with another patient in your waiting room. He said something I didn't like." The doctor later commented to his nurse, "Think of it. That cultured, intelligent woman could have blown a cerebral 'fuse' and suffered a fatal stroke—just because she didn't have forbearance with a contentious man."

Hurt feelings, anger, and grudges carry high price tags. Such emotions can backfire, causing indigestion, stomach upsets, fatigue, insomnia, and ulcers. Others may not know of our inner resentment, but the rest of our body may feel its effect.

• Envy. Envy, ill will at another's supposed superiority, is another iniquity of the interior. If unchecked, it may lash out in mean speech or malicious deeds.

Envy is that despicable twinge of delight on hearing another church is having its problems, another Sunday School is down in attendance, or another youth group has almost folded. Envy rankles when a rival is promoted or lauded. It rejoices when others weep, and weeps when others rejoice. It can't stand others having superior possessions, positions, or achievements.

The Zoo Within

In 1875 an animal lover came to Cincinnati, Ohio from New York to deliver an elephant and remained to look after it. For the next sixty-seven years he managed the zoo at Cincinnati. Yet all of us spend time managing zoos, the ones inside of us.

St. Gregory of Nyssa, who died in A.D. 395 explained how

man is mirrored in the beasts. He asked:

> Is not anger an inconsiderable beast when it barks in your heart? What is deceit when it lies hid in a cunning mind? Is it not a fox? Is not the man who is furiously bent on calumny a scorpion? Is not the person who is eagerly set on resentment and revenge a most venomous viper? What do we say of a covetous man? Is he not a ravenous wolf? Nay, there is no wild beast but is found within us.

St. Gregory then chided people for their inconsistency in subduing the animal world around, but failing to control the wild beasts within.

The Book of Romans speaks of the law of indwelling sin, an inbred principle that constantly urges man to evil and remains with him to his dying day, even after he has been regenerated (7:19-23). The noted Scottish preacher, Alexander Whyte, considered himself "the worst man in Edinburgh." He sincerely thought that if people could see into his heart, they would spit in his face.

Babylon's Hanging Gardens, one of the seven wonders of the ancient world, rose pyramidally from 1,000 feet square at the base to an apex of 400 feet high, terrace above terrace, planted with rare plants and lovely flowers. But beneath this mountain of floral beauty were the lions' dens.

A gentle facade may hide the animalistic, barbaric propensities within us. Our inner sanctums are so privately concealed that others cannot tell if we are phony or real. Deep within we can live in falseness, deciding which impressions we will make, and whether we will ever reveal our true selves.

A friend may smile and say, "Good morning, Mrs. Jones, you look wonderful." But underneath he may be thinking, "Mrs. Jones, why don't you get a different hairdo, stand up straight, and lose some weight!" Olov Hartman's *Holy Mas-*

querade is the title of a novel in which an unbelieving wife is married to a pastor. Armed with pagan honesty, she tests the quality of his faith, only to be disappointed by the hypocritical inconsistency between his public ministry and his private life.

Living Letters paraphrases Prov. 26:23, "Pretty words may hide a wicked heart, just as a pretty glaze covers a common clay."

Holy of Holies

The stable of man's depravity can become a sanctuary for the throne of God. The heart, on which the law of God was original-ly written, can be renewed in righteousness (Rom. 2:15; Eph. 4:22-24). The heart that is full of anger, malice, slander, impure thoughts, adultery, blasphemy, pride, and deceit can be changed into a heart overflowing with compassion, kindness, humility, patience, forbearance, peace, joy, and love. The Lord prom-ised, "A new heart also will I give you, and a new spirit will I put within you" (Ezek. 36:26). The following adjectives describ-ing the renewed heart indicate the possibility of transforma-tion: clean (Ps. 51:10), steadfast (Ps. 112:7), believing (Rom. 10:10), spirit-strengthened (Eph. 3:16), love-saturated (Rom. 5:5), and cleansed (Acts 15:9). The inner sanctum can be a holy of holies instead of a chamber of horrors.

This transformation begins at the new birth. By the action of the Holy Spirit, the moral base—with its bent toward evil—is given a new direction. The person who trusts the finished work of Christ on the cross becomes "a new creature," with old things passing away, and all things becoming new (2 Cor. 5:17). Then begins the process of sanctification, that gracious and continuous operation of the Holy Spirit by which He deliv-ers the pardoned sinner from the pollution of sin, renews his whole nature in the image of God, and enables him to perform good works. The holy disposition imparted in regeneration is thus maintained and strengthened. The new man progressively grows in grace.

How is the Christian sanctified? What means does the Holy Spirit use in making us more like Christ? Paul said, "Be not conformed to this world: but be transformed by the renewing of your mind" (Rom. 12:2, NASB). But how is the mind renewed? Through the Bible. Jesus said to His disciples, "You are already clean because of the word which I have spoken to you" (John 15:3, NASB). He prayed "Sanctify them through Thy truth; Thy Word is truth" (17:17, NASB). The Holy Spirit makes our inner sanctums holy through the Holy Word.

We are what we think. Since our actions are the result of our thoughts, it is absolutely essential for us to program the Word of God into our minds so that we will come to have the mind of Christ and think God's thoughts after Him. Thinking the way God thinks will help us bring every thought into captivity to Christ.

For example, let's say that I read an article or see a film in which premarital cohabitation, extramarital affairs, and cheating on one's income tax are presented as morally acceptable. If I have saturated my mind with biblical truth, I should readily reject such lifestyles as sinful. The psalmist said, "Thy word I have treasured in my heart, that I may not sin against Thee" (119:11, NASB).

Victory over the world outside comes through right thinking inside. Paul told the Ephesians, "Be renewed in the spirit of your mind" (4:23). *Living Letters* puts it, "Now your attitudes and thoughts must all be constantly changing for the better." John Stott suggests that self-control is primarily mind-control.

John Calvin said that we are to be renewed "not only with respect to the inferior appetites or desires, which are manifestly sinful, but with respect also to that part of the soul which is reckoned most noble and excellent," meaning the mind

(*Commentary on Ephesians,* Eerdmans, p. 295).

A volcano in A.D. 79 buried Pompeii under twelve feet of ashes, sealing up the entire city. Archeologists who unearthed the city 200 years ago found beautiful homes just as their owners had fled them, furniture still standing, bread in the ovens, and pet dogs still chained to the doors in the very position in which the hot ash had suddenly overtaken them.

One home was owned by a man who had painted obscene pictures on a wall in one room of his house. Apparently he kept the door shut, thinking nobody would ever know about his evil thoughts. Now the man's house has been uncovered. Guides keep the door locked so visitors won't walk in accidentally and be embarrassed. Those who wish to see can pay a small fee and gain entrance to the chamber.

It has been said, "If the best of men had his innermost thoughts written on his forehead, he'd wear a large hat and never take it off." Jesus said, "There is nothing covered, that will not be revealed; and hidden that will not be known" (Matt. 10:26, NASB).

> What if your mind were like TV,
> Where all your thoughts were plain to see?
> While others watched, what would they find—
> An honest, pure and Christlike mind,
> Or would you have to hang the sign
> Of NETWORK TROUBLE all the time?
>
> David Ravenhill

The Emperor Valentinian made this memorable deathbed statement, "Amongst all my conquests this is the only one that now comforts me. I have overcome my worst enemy, my own sinful heart."

We need to pray, "Create in me a clean heart, O God; and renew a steadfast spirit within me" (Ps. 51:10, NASB).

2
Imagine
That!

Journey into Imagination, one of the attractions at Disney-world's EPCOT center, first takes you on a simulated flight across night skies. Your host, *Dreamfinder,* a red-bearded adventurer, and his impish sidekick, a small dragon creature called *Figment* (of imagination) then guide you to *Image Works,* a fun-packed electronics factory. At a later stop, *Magic Eye Theatre,* viewers find themselves on a circus tightrope, eye to eye with somersaulting trapeze performers, and reaching out to touch birds and flowers that seem to float at arm's length. Imagination is both playful and powerful.

Imagination is an essential ingredient in man's mental capability. It is that power to form a mental image of what is not actually present, of what has never been actually experienced, or to create a new image or idea by combining previous experiences.

A *Psychology Today* article points out that the daydreaming habit is not all bad. Da Vinci's incredible machines, Newton's revolutionary theories, and much of the world's great literature and sculpture might be nonexistent if their creators had not drifted into their individual reveries (December 1982).

Inventions begin in the mind. The jet engine existed first in someone's thought. Every great structure was once a mental blueprint. The Empire State Building and the George Washington Bridge were first conceived in somebody's imagination. Michael Faraday, one of the founders of the electromagnetic theory, used to picture himself as an atom under pressure, to gain insight into the electrolyte. By dreaming about what would happen if a person could fly out into space at the speed of light, Einstein developed part of his theory of relativity.

In its literary form, the Bible involves imagination, for its truths are often stated artistically. For example, the theme of the beloved Twenty-third Psalm could have been stated factually, "God cares for His children as a good shepherd cares for his sheep." But the Holy Spirit saw fit to embellish that truth with poetic embroidery. The decorative language of the Psalm has indelibly burned the message of the shepherd's care into the hearts of untold millions the world round.

Doctors know the potential of imagination. Patients often report improvement after the use of placebos—pills which the patients mistakenly think contain medicine. A physician, diagnosing two patients the same day, found one seriously ill with poor chance of recovery, and the other with nothing medically wrong. The doctor prescribed medication for the first man and placebos for the second. A clerical error put the written diagnoses in wrong envelopes. After reading them, the very sick man recovered, while the slightly ill man became seriously ill.

A plank on the ground is easy to walk on. But few will walk the same plank if it is elevated ten feet up. When the plank is on the ground, we think of *walking.* When it's in the air, we think of *falling.* Job declared, "The thing which I greatly feared is come upon me" (3:25).

Knowing the power of suggestion, Madison Avenue's clever communicators concoct their vast advertising campaigns to appeal to our imaginations. Stores display ample quantities of enticing merchandise, including unadvertised specials, all of which lead to considerable impulse buying.

On a fishing trip Pat woke up screaming in his hotel room, "I'm suffocating! Open the window!"

His fishing partner, Mike, in the other bed, slowly emerged from a deep sleep, groggily stumbled to the window, then moaned, "I can't get it open. It's stuck!"

"Break it," Pat pleaded, "I need air."

So Mike shattered the glass with his fist.

With relief Pat sighed, "I can breathe now," then fell asleep. In the morning they discovered Mike had broken the dresser mirror.

Temptation Starts in the Imagination

Temptation may come from Satan, the world, the flesh, or from any combination of these. However, as James says, much of our temptation comes from our own sinful nature, "Every man is tempted, when he is drawn away of his own lust, and enticed. Then when lust hath conceived, it bringeth forth sin; and sin, when it is finished, bringeth forth death" (1:14-15). Note the order: desire, deed, death.

Wrongful deeds begin as inordinate desires in the mind. A burglar cases a bank, devises a plan, then holds up the bank. Every kidnapping was once a thought. Every extramarital affair was first a fantasy.

At the very beginning of Genesis we have the divine evaluation of man's thought life. "God saw that the wickedness of man was great in the earth, and that every imagination of the thoughts of his heart was only evil continually" (6:5). This is why God sent the flood. After the deluge, God promised never to again send a flood over all the world, even though "the imagination of man's heart is evil from his youth" (8:21).

Biblical history bears out the truth of man's evil imagination. When Lot saw the well-watered Jordan plain, he selfishly pitched his tent in that fertile direction. The outer eye of physical sight fed the inner eye of imagination.

Prince Shechem saw Dinah, only sister to the twelve sons of Israel, and defiled her (Gen. 34:1-2).

Joseph's brothers saw him afar off and "conspired against him to slay him," ultimately selling him into Egyptian slavery (Gen. 37:18).

Achan confessed "When I saw among the spoils a goodly Babylonish garment, and two hundred shekels of silver, and a wedge of gold of fifty shekels weight, then I coveted them, and took them" (Josh. 7:21).

From his palace roof King David "saw a woman washing herself" (2 Sam. 11:2). Even after learning she was the wife of another man, David let his imagination get the better of him; he sent for her and committed adultery.

The Lord spoke to Ezekiel in a parable of two sisters, Aholah and Aholibah, who after doting on pictures of Assyrian governors and Chaldean commanders, sent messengers to invite these men for immoral purposes (23:11ff). Jesus spoke of mental adultery and mental murder (Matt. 5:21-28).

Imagining the approval they would receive for their generosity, Ananias and Sapphira pretended to bring the full proceeds from the sale of their property, while actually withholding part for themselves. Peter recognized the source of their wrong thinking, "Why hast thou conceived this thing in thine heart?" (Acts 5:1-4)

No one falls suddenly. The arrest of a reputedly upright citizen may surprise the unsuspecting community, but he knows his public crime has been preceded by a mental landslide.

A cartoon depicted the only resident of a small, desolate island looking upward and praying, "God, I want to thank You for finally delivering me from temptation." He thought holy living could be achieved by withdrawal into a monastic sort of life. But we can never get away from ourselves. As long as we have imagination, we carry within us the source of temptation.

Stop Temptation in the Imagination

The best place to break up a huge snowball is when it's small, before it starts rolling and gets rotund. In football, the best place to break up a forward pass is by smearing the quarterback before he throws it. In hockey, the best place to break up an opponent's rush is by fore-checking him in his own end of the rink. In baseball, if a team can keep a hitter from getting to first base, he'll never score.

The Old Testament often warns against minds bent on, or plotting, or meditating mischief (Ps. 36:4; 38:12; Prov. 24:8; Isa. 32:6; Zech. 8:17). If conquered in the mind, evil will never materialize.

One Christian leader said that when an evil thought came, he found that by batting his eyelids very rapidly he broke his mental process. This voluntary act drew his attention away from the thought. Then as he caught his mental equilibrium, he would pray, "Lord, help me."

A man walking through a forest was troubled by an evil thought. Deliberately he picked up a heavy log, thus interrupting his evil train of thought and enabling him to divert his attention to asking the Lord for victory.

Jay Adams calls getting the victory at the beginning, "resistance." Because man possesses a brain, he is able to delay his response to a temptation and choose an alternate course of action. But even if a person fails to resist in its initial state, he still need not let the temptation run its full course into an act of evil. He has the Holy Spirit and the Word to help him break the chain of sin. Though it is possible through restraint to curtail the process of evil along its course, the preferable alternative is to resist evil before it gets going (*The Christian Counselor's Manual,* Baker, p. 197).

A well-known maxim says, "Sow a thought; reap an act. Sow an act; reap a habit. Sow a habit; reap a character. Sow a character; reap a destiny." Since there's destiny in thought be careful what you think! But how can you get victory in your imagination in the early stage? Here are some suggestions.

• Don't flirt with temptation. A hunter spotted a bear and raised his rifle to shoot. The bear cried out, "Can't we talk this over like two intelligent beings?" The hunter lowered his gun. Said the bear, "You want a fur coat, and I want a dinner. I'm sure we can get together sensibly on this." So they sat down and came to an agreement. Suddenly there was a commotion. After a few minutes the bear got up—all alone. The compromise had been worked out. The bear had secured his dinner, and the hunter was inside his fur coat.

A proverb says, "When you're looking at your neighbor's melon patch, you can't keep your mouth from watering, but you can run." Another puts it, "He who would not enter the room of sin must not sit by the door of temptation."

A mother reluctantly gave permission to her ten-year-old son to take a look at an old swimming pool on a warm spring day, but gave him strict orders to stay out of the water. When she returned, his hair was wet. He explained, "I fell in." When she asked why his clothes were dry, he replied, "I took off my clothes because I had a feeling I was going to fall in."

The psalmist prayed, "Turn away mine eyes from beholding vanity" (119:37). When Satan appealed to Jesus' imagination by showing Him all the kingdoms of this world, offering them to Him in return for obeisance, Jesus said, "Get thee behind Me, Satan" (Luke 4:8).

Don't dally with temptation, but deny it at the very beginning.

• Don't feed temptation. A proverb says, "You cannot keep
the birds from flying over your head, but you can keep them
from building nests in your hair." Sometimes new Christians
are concerned because evil thoughts flit across their minds. To
prevent such thoughts from parading across your imagination
may be impossible but you are certainly responsible for thoughts
you select from the passing panorama for consideration and
cherishing. To admire a woman for her beauty, or a man for
his handsomeness, is perfectly natural. What is wrong is for the
look to be accompanied by lust. The first look is not sin; the
look that leads to lust is the culprit (Matt. 5:28).

Your mind is a reception room for all kinds of thoughts—
good, bad, and indifferent. Whatever thoughts you welcome
inside this room will ultimately determine your character and
conduct.

> It's not what we think we are,
> but what we think, we are.

A sullied thought does not soil the soul, if given no room.
Rather, rejection of a wrong thought strengthens you to throw
off later evil suggestions. A passing impure thought, unwel-
comed, is not sinful, but an entertained impure desire is.

We must not feed lust by dwelling on wrong desires. The
farther down the road a person travels through dirty books,
erotic magazines, x-rated films, and filthy fantasies, the harder
it will be to stop short of sin. A *Psychology Today* survey
reported that 69 percent of the men who go to the beach go
to watch the scantily clothed women (December 1982, p. 10).
This certainly is not a wise practice for any man wishing to get
victory in his imagination. As long as temptation is just knock-

ing outside the door, you have not sinned. But when temptation enters and discusses with the mind, entices the affections,
and debates with the heart, you have entered into temptation.

A man who was severely tempted every time he walked past
a pornographic bookstore decided to take a different street
home. At a recent youth pastors' convention, the headquarters
hotel reported the highest record of x-rated movie rentals in its
history. These youthful Christian leaders were dangerously
flirting with temptation.

As Potiphar's wife cast her eyes on handsome Joseph, she
let her imagination get out of hand (Gen. 39:6-7). In those early
stages of temptation she should not have let her eyes linger in
his direction, and should have dismissed the thought as unwor-
thy of the wife of Potiphar. But entertaining the immoral idea
led to propositioning Joseph.

Amnon's rape of his half-sister, Tamar, came from his failure
to nip his imagination at the start (2 Sam. 13:1ff). How fitting
the warning: "Lust not after her (the other woman's) beauty in
thine heart" (Prov. 6:25).

Ahab's coveting of Naboth's vineyard led to the latter's murder. Instead of sulking over his desire for Naboth's land, Ahab
should have said no to his simmering covetousness in its incipi-
ent stage.

Let us learn from the patriarch Job who did not harbor
wicked imaginations, but rather said, "I made a covenant with
mine eyes; why then should I think upon a maid?" He spoke
of victory in his heart at the start (31:1, 7).

• Avoid idleness. Though at times we all need to relax, take
vacations, and enjoy recreation, we should usually be occupied
in regular work. Says the proverb, "An idle mind is the devil's
workshop." God seems to call His servants when they're busy,
like Peter from fishing, Matthew from tax-collecting, and Amos
from shepherding. In "The Cotter's Saturday Night," Robert
Burns says,

> An' mind your duty, duly, morn an' night,
> Lest in temptation's path we gang astray.

Paul wanted younger widows to remarry lest in idleness they wander as busybodies from house to house (1 Tim. 5:13). When overzealous saints at Thessalonica gave up their jobs because they thought the Lord was returning momentarily, Paul charged them with disorderly walk and ordered them to work with their hands instead of their tongues (2 Thes. 3:11-12). Paul knew that the devil finds work for idle hands to do.

Had David been leading his troops in the siege of Rabbah, instead of leisuring at Jerusalem, he would not have gotten involved with Bathsheba (2 Sam. 11:1).

The virtuous woman of Proverbs 31 was a busy lady, leaving little time for evil thoughts. Will Rogers once said, "What this country needs is dirtier fingernails and cleaner minds."

• Fill your mind with good thoughts. Victory in your thinking involves more than mere rejection of mental garbage and avoidance of idleness. Your mind can never remain a vacuum. Jesus told the story of an unclean spirit who, cast out of a house and later finding it empty, brought back seven other more wicked demons. A mere eviction of unhealthy thoughts will only open the door for far worse occupants. It is necessary not only to cast down every vain thought but also to bring in new patterns of thinking.

Sublimation is psychological jargon for directing energies and impulses away from their primitive aim to one that is ethically or culturally higher. An example—diverting the vitality of teenagers from gang warfare by channeling them into football or baseball.

Suppose an office worker sees a company executive walk into his plush office and thinks, "He's got money, position, and security. Boy, would I like his job. Perhaps I can invent a way to pull the rug out from under him and move up in the company and take his place." A positive alternative would be, "Lord, bless that executive in his work. I thank You I have a job, for it supports my family. Help me do my best, and perhaps some day You'll help me get promoted to an executive position in this company." A potentially ugly thought has been transformed into a noble, commendable desire.

To think such thoughts requires saturation in the Book which is full of lofty thoughts. Day by day, hide God's Word in your heart, so you will not sin against Him. Paul said to think on whatsoever things are true (dependable), honest (noble), just (fair), pure (unsoiled), lovely (loveable), commendable, excellent, and praiseworthy (Phil. 4:8). Such daily renewal will help make your inner sanctum a holy of holies instead of a chamber of horrors.

• Use imagination constructively. Anticipate the temptations that will come your way and invent a strategy of victory in advance. Joseph must have developed a design by which to face Potiphar's wife's repeated propositioning. His game plan was to first point out to her that such conduct on his part would be disloyal to both his master and God. Then if her solicitations persisted, he would flee, which he did. His advance use of imagination helped in his triumph over temptation.

A man with a definite weight problem, invited to a smorgasbord which always offered an assortment of rich desserts, knew that normally he would return a second and third time to sample more delicacies. So he planned a course of action. He would go to the dessert table only once, deliberately select one item, then return to his table and eat it leisurely. And that would be it. At the smorgasbord, with his intention well in mind, he was able to get victory over his weakness.

Phobias can be overcome through constructive use of imagination. You identify what you want to happen, list steps through which you will approach your fear. By use of visual imagery, you handle each stage of the situation ahead of time. Through this method many have mastered fears of flying, of height, of darkness.

How do parents go about removing dangerous objects from the reach of little toddlers? A doctor on *Good Morning, America* suggested that parents get down on their hands and knees, crawl around the house and note poisonous, breakable or injurious items, and then remove them. They were to imagine themselves seeing the house in the same way their children did. (He advised doing the crawling when neighbors aren't looking!)

A few days before his son would be driving into Boston for the first time without his parents, Dr. Gordon MacDonald took him on a dry run on the Massachusetts Turnpike over the route he would travel with his date. Even feigning a flat tire, he had his son pull quickly over to the side, get the necessary equipment from the trunk, and jack up the car. Every emergency was anticipated.

Worrying is directly related to imagination. When someone is late, how quickly we react, "Perhaps they've been in a terrible accident." We should discipline our imagination to react, "They'll be along any minute. They've just been delayed a little."

We can also use imagination in visualizing positive solutions for advancing the kingdom of God. A great evangelist dreamed of a school for training Christian workers—Moody Bible Institute became a reality. Bill Bright pictured college-age missionaries on all the major universities of our land—Campus Crusade has influenced thousands of young people for Christ all over the world.

A Christian worker gets a vision of reaching the masses through radio and TV—before long his program is carried on dozens of stations from coast to coast. A businessman sees the possibility of a film ministry—the result is a Christian cinema showing uplifting films several nights of the week. A lady imagines a strategy of reaching women through luncheons, a man of preaching to the masses in the open air, another person of influencing children. Thus we have Christian Women's Clubs, Open Air Campaigners, and Child Evangelism. The list will go on and on as God's people indulge in the sanctified use of their imagination. Without vision, people and projects perish.

Dorothy Sayers wrote, "Faith is imagination actualized by the will." Imagination can be used in prayer. Visualize the person for whom you are praying as receiving what you are asking. Picture that person a believer, or a Christian worker, or whatever you asked the Lord to make him. Imagination can picture Christian objectives and ideals it wants to reach. Though the way to actualization seems long and arduous, imagination can enlist energy and perseverance in the pursuit by keeping a clear vision of the goals. With eternity's values in view, we set our affection on things above, and lay up treasure in heaven. Thus we walk, not by sight, but by the imagination of faith.

No wonder we are to keep our heart with all diligence; for out of it are the issues of life (Prov. 4:23).

3
Garbage In—
Garbage Out

During a recent ten-month school year, a Canadian elementary pupil read over 96,000 pages from 405 library books. She was one of eighty-four pupils who read a combined total of 1,624,714 pages. Their club, designed to produce voracious readers, certainly met its goal, with an average of more than 1,900 pages per month per pupil.

Reading Is a Glorious Privilege

The Bible doesn't say much about reading, probably because scrolls were expensive and not found in most homes. Also, printing wasn't invented till the fourteenth century. However, Moses wrote the words of the Law in a book (Deut. 31:24). Ancient kings kept records of memorable deeds (Esther 6:1). The prophets wrote their messages in books. Paul asked Timothy to bring to his lonely jail some books he had left behind at Troas (2 Tim. 4:13). The Lord thought it important to put His revelation in written form, so gave us the Bible.

Reading is to the mind what exercise is to the body. Good

books stretch mental muscles. No person ever dies with a totally used brain, for no one ever exercises all his mental muscles. A person without formal schooling can secure a profound education simply by reading. A major part of a college education involves a supervised reading program. Reading permits us to pick the keenest brains of the centuries.

With the arrival of TV, some predicted the demise of book publishing. In 1971 a symposium dealing with the "doom of the book" was held in Zurich, Switzerland and drew some 300 European and American intellectuals. If books seemed doomed, however, publishers knew nothing of it. Today books are selling at an all-time high. TV, supposed to hasten the death of books, has helped to promote book reading. Thousands of libraries across the North American continent and Great Britain are linked by a giant computer network, permitting students in small colleges anywhere to borrow almost any desired book.

Much of our world's illiteracy is disappearing. Three million people, including youngsters in the bush, are learning to read every week. Some evangelical statesmen believe the most enduring work in missions comes through literacy programs.

It's hard to believe that 25 million Americans cannot read, and that another 35 million are functionally illiterate, or unable to read beyond a fifth-grade level. An estimated 74 percent of adult Americans never read a single book from one year to the next. Termed "aliterates," these people know how to read but never look between the covers of a book, seldom glance beyond the newspaper headlines, and search only for pictures in magazines. A recent *New York Times* article urged parents to read to their preschool children just fifteen minutes a day to help instill early the desire to read.

Despite this disinterest, to the making of books there is no end. Newsstands, bookstores, and libraries confront us everywhere. On a commuter train to a metropolitan city one summer morning, I suddenly became aware that practically every person on board was reading a newspaper, magazine, or book. We have rows of books in our homes. Books are great company, providing information, discovery, entertainment, inspiration, and stimulation. Many like to curl up with some volume near a fireplace to enjoy literary friendship. Reading is a grand pleasure as well as a glorious privilege.

Much Reading Material Is Pornographic

A few years ago I was in the office of the president of a Christian publishing firm. He had just come from a secular publisher's meeting in New York City and he reported remarks made by various executives. Said one publisher, "I wouldn't dare take the books I accept home for my family to read." Another, "The two important events in life are birth and death. From now on all books we publish will deal with rape or murder." Yet another editor told how a writer handed him a manuscript, exclaiming, "Print it as it is. Don't put a blue line through any of it. I know it's filthy, but both of us need the money!"

According to *Religious Broadcasting* (May 1983, p. 17), the pornography business in the U.S. grosses $6 billion a year. It is also estimated that there are between 15,000 and 20,000 "adult" bookstores in the U.S., that the number of pornographic magazine titles in print is more than 400, that 20 percent of the 6 million video cassettes sold in 1981 were porn films and that over 100 new porn films are produced each year for the 800 "adult" theaters. Our nation is inundated with a flood of vile poison, easily available to high schoolers and violating every standard of decency. Writers of "sex pulps" are often druggists, airline pilots, or housewives—"respectable" people. A California English instructor has written more than 100 salacious paperback novels in the last three years. Plots center on unbelievable characters who indulge in most every form of sexual activity with countless partners.

Some well-known novels are often defended as works of art that possess integrity and redeeming social value. And they may well be. But evidence exists that the parts of many such books which are read over and over are not the sections of literary value, but the juicy parts. One author, who threatened to publish a bibliography of titillating pages in legitimately published novels under the title of "Show Me the Good Part," said finding the passionate sections was easy. In a public library he would see a dark stripe at the edge of the book where it had been read and reread. Opening it up, he would find a sexy part. Sometimes he would just put the book down on a table and let it fall open. Again, a smutty section. Or a book with pages ripped out would almost always be a sure sign. When he secured another copy, those pages would contain salacious material. He facetiously predicted his book would help librarians know where to look to find damaged pages. Looking into much contemporary "litter-ature" is like going through a trash barrel.

Reading Can Influence Us Wrongly

Frank C. Laubach, pioneer of modern literacy programs, commented, "The man who first said, 'Tell me what you read and I will tell you what you are,' spoke a profound truth. What people see or hear twenty to fifty times they begin to believe. Soon they are practicing what they believe to be true."

Laubach related that when Lenin took over Russia, he was convinced the people would never believe communism unless indoctrinated through the printed page. So he required every man, woman, and child in Russia to become literate. In a few years the literacy rate soared from 13 percent to 90 percent. Everything the Russians were given to read taught or implied that a communist plan would be best for everybody. Severe censorship kept all else out. As a result, most Russians became convinced that theirs was the best form of government.

Americans too are molded by what they read. With smut factories churning out millions of obscene pieces of literature every month, what a harvest our nation will some day reap! The late Harvard professor, Pitirim Sorokin, wrote in his book, *The American Sex Revolution,* "At the present time the magnificent house built by western man is crumbling" (Porter Sargent Publisher).

Though some psychologists claim the effect of such litera-ture on youthful minds is minimal, many others link perusal of erotic literature with a resurgence of venereal disease, the climbing rate of illegitimacy, and violent crime. A former De-troit police inspector said, "There hasn't been a sex murder in the history of our department in which the killer was not an avid reader of lewd magazines."

Reading filth drenches the mind with pictures of obscenity, encouraging mental adultery which may be followed by actual immorality. Committing adultery behind the shades of the mind may never get mention in newspapers and statistics, but the omniscient God sees what we think.

A visitor at a chocolate plant in Hershey, Pennsylvania watched as milk and chocolate were poured into vats and came out as Hershey bars, automatically wrapped. If the work-men, instead of pouring in milk and chocolate, dumped the slop pails from local restaurant kitchens, would the result have been chocolate bars? We cannot pour junk into our minds and expect the end product to be sweet. A familiar computer slo-gan says, "GI-GO." "Garbage in—garbage out."

What About TV

Since much mental input through the eye comes from TV, perhaps a word on television would fit at this spot, especially since the average person spends more time watching TV than reading books. Studies show that the TV set is on more than 8 hours a day in the average home. By graduation from high school, today's typical teenager has spent 15,000 hours before the set. Perfect attendance in Sunday School would total less than 1,000 hours. During that same period he has been exposed to 350,000 commercials, and has observed 18,000 dramatized murders. According to a Nielson survey, over 6 million children between 2 and 11 are watching TV at 10 P.M. One million of them are still glued to the set at 1 A.M.

Children who are heavy TV watchers are often the poorest students, overly aggressive, unable to concentrate, insensitive to others' pain, unimaginative, lacking in reading ability and incentive. Excessive turning on of the set turns off the process of growing up properly. TV's successful techniques of short segments, sudden cuts, and speedy action all condition the brain to fast change but not to concentration of thought. A child raised on TV can vegetate, and become a stranger to his parents, friends, and serious learning.

TV not only mirrors society, but also functions as a model for values and behavior. A decade ago researchers held that TV's negative effects were minimal, mainly affecting those who already had psychological or social problems. Now a shifting consensus acknowledges that TV does shape attitudes. To be bombarded with cohabitation, homosexuality, wife-swapping, adultery, rape, nudity, prostitution, and violence—as acceptable and seemingly desirable behavior—can only produce widespread, damaging repercussions. Think of the influence of cable TV. Along with its excellent programs, it can bring its 24 million American home-subscribers both soft and hard-core porn movies with all their moral filth. TV is a momentous and unparalleled force in shaping our lives.

A study of leading TV writers and Hollywood executives reveals that 51 percent do not regard adultery as wrong, 80 percent do not consider homosexuality wrong, 97 percent favor abortion as a private choice, and 93 percent never or rarely attend a religious service. Their lifestyle is bound to bias their productions.

So often a Christian exclaims of something on the screen, "Isn't that awful!" and then proceeds to watch. If the 40 million people in the U.S. who claim to be born again would turn their dials off during sleezy programs, the ratings would drop and so would the sponsors. One father, sensing the hold TV had on his family, yanked the TV cord. Then he allowed each member of the family to select one hour per week, and to also watch the others' hour-long choices. This rationing slowly lessened their dependence on TV and gave a new impetus to family togetherness. They discussed the programs they watched from a moral perspective: this helped the children to understand the reasons for their choices.

Reading Can Have a Positive Influence

A mother was shocked one evening to hear her oldest son remark, "When I'm grown, I'm going to find a hideout in the mountains and rob banks and rich guys!" Before she could reply, her younger boy exclaimed, "Not me! I'm going to be a medical missionary in Africa." The first boy had been reading comic books about Mountain Ridge bandits, while the other loved the books in the Jungle Doctor series which told how a Christian doctor helped people in Africa. Of course, dozens of other influences would sweep into the lives of these brothers before they finalized their choice of careers. But books can wield an impact for good or for evil.

John Newton, in his nefarious days as infidel and libertine, nearly lost his life in a severe storm at sea. Just prior to the storm this slave-dealing sailor—destined to be a pastor as well as author of "Amazing Grace"—had been reading Thomas a Kempis' *The Imitation of Christ.* As a result, he asked himself over and over, "What if these things are true?" Both book and storm were factors in his conversion.

In *Heroic Colonial Christians,* author Russell Hitt traces the impact of the book, *The Life and Diary of David Brainerd* by Jonathan Edwards, on the lives of so many well-known Christian leaders including John Wesley, William Carey, Henry Martyn, Robert Murray McCheyne, Robert Morrison, David Living-stone, Francis Asbury, and right down to Auca-martyr Jim Elliot, whose own journal specifically mentions Brainerd's *Diary.*

T. J. Bach, founder of TEAM, was converted through a tract handed him on a Copenhagen street. When he was offered the tract, he made a discourteous remark, then crumpled the paper in his pocket. Later he unraveled the paper, read the message, and gave his heart to Christ. That night he sought out a church service where he confessed Christ. Untold numbers who have been blessed by tracts, articles, and books, have given vast sums of money to support Christian causes, and have themselves responded to Christian service, foreign and home. Chuck Colson cites as a major factor in his conversion the reading of C. S. Lewis' *Mere Christianity.*

Some Suggestions for Reading

Reading wisely is part of loving God with your mind. But with 50,000 titles published in 1983, plus the thousands already on the market, what should you read? Here are some suggestions.

• Exercise self-censorship. Though every now and again we hear of some successful attempt to rid a locality of lewd literature, many antipornographic crusades seem nothing more than efforts in futility, mainly because of the elusive definition of prurient material. Since we cannot barge into stores or libraries and tear up books we deem immoral, perhaps we would better expend effort on self-censorship. Instead of burning books belonging to others, we should ban from our personal perusal those works which titillate and entice us toward evil.

Of course, words are neither moral nor immoral. What is crucial is what happens when they are absorbed and transformed into behavior. Deep within each of us is a mixture of impulses, good and bad, waiting to be stimulated or discouraged by outer influences. The effect of some stimuli is to awaken impulses that lead to deception, greed, lust, or hate. We should ever be cautious about the moral influences to which we subject ourselves. Too often a second look leads to lingering looks and then to reading. The minute we find a book feeding wrong desires we should exercise self-censorship. The practice of this outer control will lead to inner control.

A medical doctor in London accepted Christ during a Billy Graham crusade. In keeping with his lifestyle, his reading room was crammed with salacious literature and suggestive pictures. But after his conversion, he found such literature repulsive. So he gathered up the obscene material, carried it to London Bridge, and threw it into the Thames River. As a new Christian, putting off "the old man" with its sinful deeds required the self-censorship of removing any literature that pampered his old ways.

An interesting, unofficial poll of campus post offices in Christian colleges found *Time* and *Newsweek* received by more students than any other magazine. *Sports Illustrated* placed third, with *Psychology Today* and *Christianity Today* tied for fourth. These were followed by *Glamour, Campus Life, Mademoiselle,* and *His.* On secular campuses nationally, a Chicago research firm found *Playboy, Time,* and *Newsweek* the most read magazines. The exclusion of *Playboy* from Christian college post offices seems to exhibit some degree of self-censorship, though some of these Christian students may have made newsstand purchases.

• Read discriminately. Some Christians think that reading any non-Christian book is dangerous. This view is held by many cults who wish their adherents to read only from an approved list. But as Christians we know that all truth is God's truth. Because knowledge of truth provides the best defense against heresy, it is necessary to expose ourselves to the alternate points of view so that we can cultivate the ability to analyze thought systems and thus recognize error.

If a book contains a scene depicting sex or violence or uses profanity, this does not make it immoral. Whether or not a story is obscene depends on how and why it is told. If recounted to excuse wrongdoing or to inflame the imagination, it is immoral. If told to show the wrongness of sin or its evil consequences, it is morally wholesome. Such is the purpose of the Bible, against which so often the charge of immorality has been leveled because the Bible contains so-called "x-rated" stories like that of David and Bathsheba.

The Bible's plain speaking has undoubtedly kept many from yielding to sensual temptation and has rescued others from vices. How different from vulgar books which play up sexual abuse with the most lurid and minute particulars, at the same time making it appear commendable and desirable. Whereas the pulps utilize several juicy sentences to dwell on immoral acts, the Bible keeps its distance, speaking of the act with great reserve in an unembellished sentence or two. Just like a medical textbook which deals with the structure and illnesses of the human body, so the Bible is God's book on moral anatomy and spiritual disease. If the so-called impure stories were omitted, the Bible would be gapingly defective in its handling of the moral dangers and spiritual plagues that beset mankind.

Obviously, if we are to address ourselves seriously to the culture of our day, we must break out of the routine of reading the same few magazines, newspapers, and authors, and acquaint ourselves with secular literature in its different perspectives. In doing so we should take note of the world view from which beliefs and behaviors are presented. Does the author believe in a personal, infinite God? Does he believe that man is distinguished from and superior to the animals? That he is made in the image of God? Does the author hold that man fell from his original estate and became a sinful creature? That man's only hope is in the redemption provided through Christ Jesus who entered the stream of history 2,000 years ago? If the answer to these questions is yes, then the book is probably expressing a Christian viewpoint. But if cohabitation before marriage, homosexuality, or adulterous affairs are tolerated frivolously or nonjudgmentally, or if there is ridicule of those who uphold a moral position, the material is expressing an immoral bias and is potentially deleterious.

• Read widely. It goes without saying that we ought to read the Bible regularly. Also, we ought to devote a good share of our reading time to Christian books. But beyond that, there are many guides to good reading. *The Great Books of the Western World,* selected by Mortimer Adler and Robert Hutchins, includes 443 works by writers from the early Greeks to the early twentieth century. *The Harvard Classics,* covering the same period, edited by a former Harvard president, aims to provide the foundation "essential to the twentieth-century idea of a cultivated man." In *How to Read Slowly,* James W. Sire ends with an *Appendix: Reading with a Plan,* aimed at understanding various current world views (InterVarsity). Anthologies, bestseller lists, and book reviews provide good suggestions, though sometimes they tell which books people *are* reading rather than those which people *ought to* read.

A mother was peeling vegetables for a salad when her daughter, home from college for a semester break, casually mentioned she was going to a movie that night. "I know it's x-rated, but several friends are going." The mother suddenly picked up a handful of garbage and threw it in the salad. "Mother!" said the shocked girl. "You're putting garbage in the salad!"

"I know," replied the mother, "but I thought that if you didn't mind garbage in your mind, you certainly wouldn't mind a little in your stomach!"

Reading can make our inner sanctum either a garden or jungle, a holy place or a horror chamber.

4
Christian Meditation

For a while, TM (Transcendental Meditation) was the best known self-help therapy in America. Called a drugless high and the turn-on of the 1970s, it demanded only that its devotees sit still for twenty minutes each morning and evening and silently repeat their individually assigned mantras. Adherents claimed that meditating twice a day would cure almost everything from high blood pressure to drug addiction. However, TM lost popularity when it was shown to be permeated with a Hindu world view.

Though we tend to associate TM and other forms of meditation with mystics and monks, meditation was a biblical exercise. "Isaac went out to meditate in the field at the eventide" (Gen. 24:63). David asked the Lord, "Consider my meditation" (Ps. 5:1). After giving instructions to Timothy, Paul said, "Meditate upon these things" (1 Tim. 4:15). The Lord specifically commanded Joshua, as he succeeded Moses, "This book of the Law shall not depart out of thy mouth; but thou shalt meditate therein day and night" (Josh. 1:8). The blessed man

delights in the precepts of the Lord; "in His law doth he meditate day and night" (Ps. 1:2). Meditation is not an option but
an obligation. We are commanded not only to pray and praise,
but also to *ponder,* setting our minds on things above (Col. 3:2).

What is Christian Meditation?

• It involves the mind. So much that passes for meditation
rules out the use of the mind. In one type of so-called contemplation you take a parable or sentence, close out the outside
world, and think, usually coming out with little or nothing. In
another type you simply concentrate on one spot, perhaps on
the wall or on your navel. In TM you empty your mind, switching it into neutral, repeating your Sanskrit mantra, a meaning-
less sound that supposedly will help your mind reach a quiet
state. But all these practices inhibit rather than stimulate
meditation.

Christian meditation requires reflection, contemplation, study.
Meditation comes from a Latin verb *meditari,* meaning "to
ponder or weigh." The Greek verb translated "meditate" in
1 Tim. 4:15 means "to bestow careful thought on, to give
careful attention to, to be earnest in." The Hebrew verb for
meditate means "murmuring," giving the picture of a person
mumbling to himself, not in the negative aspect of complain-
ing, but rather with the positive idea of contemplating the
goodness of God.

• It involves the sustained use of the mind. Christian meditation demands sustained reflection, continuous application of
the mind to some truth. Many figures of speech have been
utilized to describe this quality, like the squeezing of juice out
of fruit, hens setting on eggs to keep them warm till hatching,
kindling a fire under green wood, or the pounding of incense
to make it odoriferous, or the extraction of honey from flowers
by bees. Philip Henry said, "A garment that is doubled-dyed,

dipped again and again, will retain the color a great while; so a truth which is the subject of meditation" (*Leadership,* Winter '84, p. 86).

The most graphic picture of meditating is that of chewing the cud. Many animals, including sheep, cattle, goats, camels, and giraffes, are classified *ruminant.* That's because they have stomachs with four compartments, the first of which is called the *rumen.* In its digestive process, a cow bolts its food down in concentrated eating, much like a lawncutter mowing grass. Then a little while later, she reclines in a shady spot and regurgitates the food out of her rumen. This time she chews the food thoroughly so that it proceeds to the second, third, and fourth compartments, and is finally digested into the animal's bloodstream.

A man once timed a ruminating cow. Lying by a stream, the cow regurgitated some grass, chewed it for 55 seconds, swallowed it, then brought up another bite. For several minutes the cow never varied its 55-second length of rumination.

To meditate is to ruminate. Like cud-chewing, pondering God's truth gives us nourishment for our spiritual bloodstream.

• It involves the Scriptures. Za-Zen, ancient Buddhist form of meditation, means "just sitting." As the postulant adopts an alert, simple, seated position, he pays attention to rhythmic breathing. Any thoughts that enter the mind are to be observed, but quick return should be made to concentration on sitting and breathing. Though this inner tranquility may give rise to flashes of intuition, this practice can in no sense be considered Christian meditation.

Performers under tension have long used meditative rituals to reduce stress and restore inner balance. Likewise, composers and writers have engaged in meditation to aid concentration and release imagination. But impulses reaching out to the gods are vague, unorthodox, and in no way resemble Christian meditation.

Nor is Christian meditation the mindless repetition of some secret formula, the chanting of some phrase over and over, or blank staring at some object. To qualify as Christian meditation, the object of contemplation must be a definite body of truth—the Scriptures. Any theme in God's Word is a legitimate subject for meditation.

In his book *Christian Meditation,* Dr. Edmund P. Clowney mentions three dimensions of Christian meditation that reveal its distinctiveness, and offer guidance in its practice. Christian meditation is rooted in the *truth* of God, is a response to the *love* of God, and is an exercise in *praise* to God (Craig Press, p. 9).

The 119th Psalm, the longest chapter of that book, is an acrostic meditation on the Word of God. For everyone of the twenty-two letters of the Hebrew alphabet the psalmist has composed eight verses, with all 176 centering his mind on the statutes of God. Such rumination delighted his soul. "O how love I Thy law! It is my meditation all the day" (v. 97).

Mary, the mother of Jesus, must have meditated much on the Old Testament. Her Magnificat shows her saturation in Scripture, as she alluded to several Old Testament books including 1 Samuel, Psalms, Isaiah, Micah, and Exodus.

In *Knowing God* Dr. James I. Packer says:

Meditation is a lost art today, and Christian people suffer grievously from their ignorance of the practice. Meditation is the activity of calling to mind, and thinking over, and dwelling on, and applying to oneself, the various things that one knows about the works and ways and purposes and promises of God. It is an activity of holy thought, consciously performed in the presence of God, under the eye of God, by the help of God, as a means of communion with God. Its purpose is to clear one's mental and spiritual vision of God, and to let His truth make its full and proper impact on one's mind and heart (InterVarsity, pp. 18-19).

Helps on Meditation

One reason many like TM is that it promises to do so much with so little fuss and bother. Its leaders claim that a few months of meditation by one-tenth of the world's adults would usher in global peace, empty all hospitals, and banish poverty and crime. Except for the twenty minutes twice a day, its practice causes practically no personal inconvenience, no repentance of past misdeeds, and no demands of future godly living. Man's sin problem and its cure through Jesus' death on the cross are ignored.

Christian meditation not only bathes deeply in the sacrifice of Christ and His glorious resurrection; it also demands discipline. The meditator must have a strong desire to know God as He is revealed in both written and incarnate Word. And he also must learn to concentrate.

• Have a regular time. Some suggest a minimum of five days a week, perhaps to avoid the legalistic trap of a daily "must." However, many Christian leaders believe we should make a commitment to meditate every day, claiming that just as we need physical food every day, so we need daily spiritual nourishment.

Christ meditated early in the day. It was at evening that Isaac meditated. Whenever we do it, morning or evening or both, we should set aside a definite period, trying to safeguard that time slot for that purpose.

How long should you meditate? Start with five minutes. Then as you notice how quickly the time passes, increase it to ten minutes, then fifteen, and even up to half an hour. If TM requires its disciples to meditate forty minutes on a meaning-less word, should not the Lord's followers devote fifteen or twenty minutes a day to reflect on the glorious majesty of Father, Son, and Spirit?

• Cover the entire Word. Meditate systematically on the entire Word, not just Psalm 23, or the Gospel of John, or a few favorite verses or chapters, letting the rest of the Bible go by in default. Over a period of time you will have searched most of the Scriptures, from Genesis to Revelation.

Before long, you should be ruminating on deeper biblical matters. In a restaurant you'd look silly ordering a baby bottle filled with milk and covered with a sterilized nipple, while all around were eating steaks or hamburgers. Yet many Christians keep meditating on the simple milk of the Word when they should be digesting its meat.

• Ponder by paragraphs. A whole chapter may contain too many concepts for meditative purposes. On the other hand, a single verse may need a larger context for fifteen minutes of rumination. Some translations are printed in paragraph form. Such units of thought are often ideal for contemplative prac-tice. Again you may be able to cover more than one paragraph in your devotional period.

On finishing a paragraph, you may help your contemplation by asking questions such as these suggested by the late Paul Little:

Is there an example to follow, like Daniel's resolve not to defile himself with forbidden food? Have I the courage to say no in the midst of a crowd indulging in a wrong practice?

Is there a sin to avoid, like the Israelites murmuring in the wilderness? Have I been grumbling about the food recently?

Is there a command to obey, like bearing someone's burden? Have I been putting off visiting that shut-in friend?

Is there a promise to claim? Though some promises are

conditional, many are unrestricted like, "If ye abide in Me, and My words abide in you, ye shall ask what ye will, and it shall be done unto you" (John 15:7).

What does this paragraph teach me about God? Has it given me a new concept of the majesty or sovereignty or goodness of God?

Is there a difficulty to explore later? The Gospel of Matthew says two blind men were healed, but Luke just mentions Bartimaeus.

Is there someone this passage wants me to pray for, like those in authority?

Are there some things I should be thankful for, like my family, my work, my salvation?

Is there something here I should share with others? (Paul Little, *How to Give Away Your Faith,* InterVarsity, pp. 126-127).

• Recall the Word during the day. The psalmist said of the Word, "It is my meditation all the day" (119:97). Many believers have just one main meditation period each day. Some take advantage of morning and afternoon coffee breaks. One college student liked to meditate while walking from class to class. Another said, "I try to take several short meditation breaks, even if only half a minute or so. They can be most strengthening."

A college girl who volunteered to counsel at a girls' camp was given an assignment far below her ability, that of peeling potatoes in the kitchen. A friend, recognizing the situation, remarked, "It's too bad a girl of your education and talent should have to peel potatoes." The girl who was genuinely humble happily remarked, "I don't have to think about potatoes while I'm peeling them. I can think about my Bible verse for the day!"

To meditate on some Bible verse during the day at a time when it's impossible to pull out your Bible or Testament requires previous memorization of that verse. Memorizing Scripture provides a grand foundation for meditation.

• Meditation during the night. Psychologists tell us the subconscious mind works while we sleep. How often we go to bed with a problem on our mind, only to find it solved on awakening. Language students have discovered that by reviewing ten or so new vocabulary words just before retiring, their subconscious continues working on them while they sleep, so that in the morning about 60 percent are mastered.

Dawson Trotman, founder of the Navigators, believed that the last prevailing thought in one's conscious mind before going to sleep should be some portion of God's Word. He called this his H.W.L.W. principle (His Word the Last Word). Associates with whom he traveled said that at the close of day, with lights out and conversation ended, someone would quote a verse or short passage from the Bible. The theory was that this last dominant idea would simmer in the subconscious and become the first thought on rising.

If you find yourself unable to sleep, it's profitable to think on some portion of God's truth. The blessed man meditates in God's law "day and night" (Ps. 1:2). The psalmist speaks of meditating on God "in the night watches" (63:6).

• Other topics for meditation. A verse of Scripture may lead your mind to related topics, like the attributes of God—His love, grace, majesty, omniscience, sovereignty, wisdom, holiness, faithfulness, and goodness. You may muse on His works in creation and redemption. Some have received substantial blessing from reflecting on the beauty and order of our world with its flowers, starry skies, trees, mountains, oceans, and sunsets. Others have contemplated the wisdom of God in creating the wonders of the human body. Still others have considered the providence of God in history.

Meditation may lead you to take inventory of your own

spiritual condition. Are you discovering, developing, and deploying your spiritual gifts? Are you using your time wisely, giving sacrificially of your money to the support of the church and poor? And guarding your tongue in daily conversation? Such analysis may be unpleasant, but necessary to fuller obedience. Meditation may give guidance for future plans. However, too much introspection is unhealthy. Normal people do not take their pulse too often.

• Write down your meditation. Keep a spiritual notebook or journal. When a topic draws your interest, give it free reign. Don't quench the Spirit who may wish to bring forth fresh ideas, not for satisfaction of curiosity but for fruitful advance. Note lessons learned, applications to particular needs, and answered prayers.

The Psalms and Proverbs are really written meditations. Augustine's *Confessions* is basically a devotional meditation. With pen in hand, the Bishop of Hippo was contemplating before the Lord.

A daily diary will clarify your growth in understanding, so write candidly, but not indiscreetly. Why not compose prayers and poems, even if you are not talented in that area? Poems don't have to rhyme or have correct meter. Let your thoughts race unorganized. If you later deem them worthy, you can formalize them to share with friends.

One believer said, "The goal of my meditation is to write down my insights and goals in my spiritual diary, and then act on them during the day."

Benefits of Meditation

TM claims to lower the blood pressure, reduce tension, clear the mind, sweeten the disposition, and decrease dependency on drugs. However, psychology and cardiovascular researchers point out that resting fifteen minutes daily for a three-month period will have as much physical effect as TM. They also remind us that TM is nothing new, that meditation has been a way of achieving mental serenity through the ages. Christian meditation has definite advantages over other types of so-called meditation.

• It illuminates the mind. Thoughts bombard our minds even as we try to read the Bible. Meditation helps us weed out extraneous thoughts and keeps our minds from becoming fields of overgrown flowers.

Christianity involves a body of truth. Paul's epistles begin with doctrinal content. Paul persuaded, reasoned, taught. By meditation we come to understand the intellectual substance of our faith. "The entrance of Thy words giveth light; it giveth understanding unto the simple" (Ps. 119:130).

Early in his ministry Martin Luther learned the necessity of meditating before preaching. Once, instead of preparing a sermon, he walked into his pulpit hoping the Lord would give him proper words to utter. Later Luther said that God had spoken to him: "Martin, you're unprepared!"

Meditation teaches lessons for life. We learn how Samson made a fool of himself over Delilah, and we profit from his negative example. We see how David was so forgiving of Saul who was seeking his life, and we hope we will be as forgiving.

Because meditation can make us more alert to our neighbors' needs, and eager to find ways to help, it can be a preparation for activism. Many solutions to problems come through the exercise of our minds in meditation.

• It strengthens the soul. Meditation stores up strength for the day of temptation. When the enemy draws near the castle of the heart he finds it well furnished to resist his assaults. The psalmist wrote, "Thy word have I hid in mine heart, that I might not sin against Thee" (119:11).

Maturity of strength does not come all at once nor through

ten easy lessons for successful Christian living. Daily rumination in divine truth will imperceptibly develop a mind-set which will act as a defense against enemy attacks. Truth so absorbed into the spiritual bloodstream will enable you to identify thought patterns which should be eradicated, like worry, pride, lust, or anger. It will also help you have victory over the subliminal seduction contained in the hundreds of advertising messages thrown at you every day.

The person who delights in God's law day and night "shall be like a tree planted by the rivers of water, that bringeth forth his fruit in his season; his leaf also shall not wither; and whatsoever he doeth shall prosper" (Ps. 1:3).

• It calms the spirit. Meditation can provide an island of calm in an ocean of distress. How often the psalmist started out in anguish, but after meditating on the character of God, ended in joy. On one occasion he began, "Lord, how are they increased that trouble me! Many are they that rise up against me." Then he thought, "But thou, O Lord, art a shield for me." He ended rejoicing, "Salvation belongeth unto the Lord" (Ps. 3:1-2, 8).

It was said that whenever Lord Cairns entered the British House of Lords, his presence seemed to bring peace and harmony. His secret, he said, was his habit of spending two hours each morning in scriptural meditation and prayer.

J. I. Packer says of meditation:

> It is, indeed, often a matter of arguing with oneself, reasoning oneself out of moods of doubt and unbelief into a clear apprehension of God's power and grace. Its effect is to encourage and reassure us . . . as we contemplate the unsearchable riches of divine mercy displayed in the Lord Jesus Christ (*Knowing God,* InterVarsity, p. 19).

God has promised to keep in perfect peace those whose minds are stayed on Him (Isa. 26:3).

• It deepens our devotion. When a girl in love receives a letter from her fiance, she reads it meditatively, then rereads every line, above the line, below the line, and between the lines. One girl spent an hour pondering the meaning of two words, "As ever," at the end of her boyfriend's letter. Someone dubbed this "devotional reading."

We love God because He first loved us. Pondering more of His person and work will foster deeper communion and will lead to prayer and praise. The many portions of prayer and praise in the Bible should be part of our meditation too. It is the Word dwelling in believers richly (meditatively) that enables them to speak to each other in psalms, hymns, and spiritual songs (Col. 3:16).

During his final illness, the noted Southern Baptist preacher and pastor of First Baptist Church, Dallas for forty-four years, Dr. George Truett, was attended by a private nurse. He would be conscious for a while, then lapse into a coma. Sometimes when unconscious, he would talk "out of his head." One day when he came to, he said to the nurse, "I haven't been conscious, have I?"

"No, you have not been conscious," the nurse replied, "but you have been talking."

Dr. Truett began to weep. "O nurse, what did I say? Even when my mind is not conscious of what I am saying, if I would say anything to bring reproach to Christ, or anything less than what a Christian ought to say, it would break my heart."

The nurse smiled, patted him on the head, and as he was about to pass over into the New Land, said, "No, Dr. Truett, I have been here with you all the time. When you spoke in your unconsciousness, you would preach a while. Then you would speak about winning a soul to Jesus. And you sang songs about Christ. Then you prayed."

Dr. Truett's lips quivered, "Oh, I'm so glad! For I want, even when not conscious, to bring glory to Him!"

We need to pray, "Let the words of my mouth, and the meditation of my heart, be acceptable in Thy sight, O Lord" (Ps. 19:14). How wonderful when His thoughts are our thoughts, and our thoughts are His.

5
Down
Memory Lane

A waiter in a fashionable Colorado restaurant takes orders without writing anything down. Once he handled a table of nineteen complete dinners without a single mistake. The menu contains sixty items—including eight steaks cooked five different ways, four salds, and several desserts. Customers have failed to fool him by switching orders. Sometimes they bet him his tip, double or nothing, that he will make an error. In four years he has lost only once.

Conductor Arturo Toscanini memorized every note for every instrument for 250 symphonies and 100 operas.

About the turn of the century, a factory worker in England was found to have a freak memory. Given the professional name Data, he played the vaudeville circuit for over thirty years. He would saunter across the stage and without strain would answer questions fired at him from all parts of the house about dates of events. He knew every one of the 50,000 dates in a dictionary of dates. Never did he give a wrong answer. Yet with all his mnemonic gifts, one night he left the theater fumbling in his pockets and mumbling, "I've forgotten where I put my gloves." They were on top of a nearby piano.

The *Wall Street Journal* featured an article on a forty-year-old editor who is called by many a "walking library." Several writers and intellectuals have come to rely on his prodigious memory to help them in their research for appropriate literary allusions, obscure historical facts, or little-remembered quotations. This Oxford-bred whiz reads sixty to seventy hours a week, sometimes spending mornings at the Library of Congress. Clients are amazed how he can recount details of history off the top of his head (21 December 1982).

The Marvel of Memory

Though the memories of these men are exceptional, the average memory does a phenomenal job of storing and recalling millions of bits of information. Its storage capacity seems limitless, with a filing system that arranges information under general headings. When you want to recall data, the memory will scan the "file" to track it down, usually taking just a fraction of a second.

An article in IBM's *THINK* magazine suggested that certain selected patterns of information are fixed or frozen into permanent records among intricate nerve-cell networks, and are stored with amazing compactness. It is estimated that the brain can hold enough data to fill several million books, making our microfilming ability seem insignificant ("How the Human Memory Functions," April 1963).

Dr. Wilder G. Penfield is one of the world's foremost brain surgeons. During an operation on a young secretary, he touched a spot on her cortex with a stimulating electrode. She said, "I hear music." When the electrode was removed, the music stopped. Fifteen minutes later the contact was placed on the same spot with the same result. "I hear music again. It's like radio." The Canadian surgeon repeated the test twenty times on an area the size of a matchhead. Each time he did, she heard the same tune, "Marching Along Together," in full instrumentation as the orchestra had played it at some past recital. It was like the reel of a submicroscopic tape unwinding in her mind. When the electrode was replaced, the music did not pick up from its previous stopping point; the mental reel automatically wound itself back to the beginning of the play-back. This rewinding process seems familiar to us; for when we try to recall a line of a song, we often find ourselves unable to repeat it unless we go back to the very beginning and proceed through the stanzas till we come to the line we want.

Though the exact workings of memory remain a puzzle, it is believed that chemical substances are very much involved. Also, there seems to be hidden away in the brain a stream of consciousness which retains all impressions in detail.

Youth has been called the golden age of memory. Neil Fich-thorn, Director of Music at Sandy Cove Bible Conference, Mary-land, counted fifty-five songs his youth choir learned in the first two months of the 1983 summer conference, an average of almost one a day. These complete songs, usually with several verses, were well remembered weeks after originally learned.

Older folks more easily recall events that happened long ago than they do the recent ones. A patient in a nursing home, when asked about an old Swedish prayer, repeated it without a hitch, to the amazement of her daughter who had never heard her mother say it once. The mother had undoubtedly learned the prayer in childhood.

Augustine wrote in his *Confessions* of "the plains, caverns, and abysses of my memory; they are innumerable kinds of things. . . . Through all this range, I fly here and I fly there; I dive down deep as I can, and I can find no end. So great is the force of memory."

Emphasis on Remembering

If the brain remembers everything to which we ever devote attention, we should be careful about what we permit to become part of our permanent mental microfilm.

The Lord repeatedly commanded Israel to remember and not forget. Likewise, God's saints today are to remember the same things about the Lord.

• The goodness and greatness of God. Israel was to remember God's majesty in saving them from bondage and in leading them through forty years of wilderness, so that their clothes did not wear out, the manna fail, nor the water diminish. God used several memorials like the Passover, manna kept in the ark of the holy of holies, three annual feasts, tassels on corners of garments, and stones from the river set up in Gilgal, to help them remember. Joshua's farewell speech reviewed God's gracious dealings (Josh. 24).

• The chastisements of God. Israel was to "remember, and forget not, how they provoked the Lord to wrath in the wilderness (Deut. 9:7). As a result of constant murmuring and unbelief, that generation never reached the Promised Land. After they returned from Babylonian exile and rebuilt the temple, the memory of the original temple's glory made them weep profusely (Ezra 3:12-13).

Jesus told His hearers to remember Lot's wife (Luke 17:32). Jude wanted his readers to remember how people, angels, and cities had fallen from privileged positions to severe judgment (Jude 5-7).

• The words of God. When the new generation of Israelites was about to enter the Promised Land, the Lord repeated all the words of the first Law given in the Book of Exodus, which they were to remember and obey. *Deuteronomy* means "second law."

More than once Jesus told His followers to recall a previously spoken word (John 15:20). He also promised that memory would help them in a coming tribulation (16:4). He gave an ordinance with visual reminders to help them remember His broken body and shed blood (1 Cor. 11:23-26).

Values of Remembering

Meditation and memorization have been called twins. Memorization of verses makes it possible to meditate after we've closed our Bibles. Memorization enables us to ponder God's truth day or night. Through the centuries most believers could neither read nor write. So they committed psalms to heart by chanting and then meditated on God's Word as they worked. Slaves in America offset their illiteracy by memorization of the Bible stories they had heard. When they committed Sunday School lesson passages to memory, they could cogitate on the spiritual truths. Meditation is the chewing and digesting of spiritual food, made possible because that food has been previously stored in the memory.

Since we are born anew by the incorruptible seed of the Word of God (1 Peter 1:23), verses learned from memory can lead to salvation. As Martin Luther climbed the steps of Sacra Scala in Rome, thereby hoping to cut time from purgatory, like a shaft of light in a dark night he remembered the text, "The just shall live by faith" (Rom. 1:17). In a surge of freedom, he stood up and walked back down the steps.

If our memories dredge up the vileness of past sins, pertinent memorized verses can remind us that God has placed our sins out of His sight (behind His back) and out of His mind (to be remembered no more) (see Ps. 103:12; Col. 2:13; 1 John 1:9). If God has forgotten them, so should we. As a former enemy, persecutor, blasphemer, and murderer of believers, Paul knew the nightmare of memories that could have paralyzed his ministry. But he said he forgot those things which were behind and pressed on to things in the future (Phil. 3:13-14).

Since positive thinking usually leads to thanking, godly remembering can lead to worship. A professed atheist asked why he should thank God for his food, when he earned it through his own work. The answer came, "To labor with your hands requires health, strength, and a body capable of coordination. Besides, you need proper oxygen content in the air, temperature to sustain human life, and the sun to give healthful rays!"

Israel was exhorted not to think it had earned prosperity through its own initiative, ingenuity, or industry (Deut. 8:17-19). Pondering that it is God who gives us the strength to acquire our material possessions will lead us to worship His great Name, and will help to keep us from grumbling. How soon after some great blessing the Israelites forgot and began to murmur.

Memory of divine facts can lead us to be kind to others. The Israelites in the Promised Land were more likely to treat aliens better when they recalled their own days of slavery in Egypt (Deut. 15:15; 24:17-18, 22).

It's interesting to note how often the memory is spoken of in connection with kindness. Paul was exhorted to remember the poor (Gal. 2:10) and admonished the Colossians to remember his bonds (Col. 4:18). The writer of Hebrews asked his readers, "Remember them that are in bonds, as bound with them" (13:3). Prison ministries today are led by those who remember these enjoinders.

After their early zeal for the Lord, the Ephesian Christians let complacency rob them of their first love. John wrote to them, "Remember therefore from whence thou art fallen, and repent, and do the first works" (Rev. 2:5).

If someone, formerly active in Christian work, but now without warmth of spirit for the Lord, will relive those initial days of dedication, this remembering will be a big step toward restoration. The memory of the plenty of his father's home helped the prodigal decide to go home. The crowing of the cock alerted Peter's memory to his Master's prediction of denial. Part of the torture of hell for the rich man was in remembering his mistreatment of the beggar who had sat at his gate.

A major benefit of memorizing particular Bible verses is the strengthening of the Christian life. When Jesus was tempted by the devil, He began His answer each time the same way, "It is written," then quoted a verse from Deuteronomy to counter Satan's ruse (compare Luke 4:3-12; Deut. 8:3; 6:13, 16).

Two carousing men, noticing a young lad on board their ocean liner, agreed that they should persuade him to take a drink of liquor. Approaching the boy pleasantly, one of the men invited him to come and have a glass of wine.

"Thank you, Sir," said the boy, "but I never drink intoxicating liquor."

"Never mind, my lad; it won't hurt you. Please do come and have a drink with me."

" 'Wine is a mocker, strong drink is raging: and whosoever is deceived thereby is not wise,' " (Prov. 20:1) was the boy's reply.

"You need not be deceived by it. I wouldn't have you drink much. A little will do you no harm but just liven you up."

" 'At the last it biteth like a serpent, and stingeth like an adder,' " (Prov. 23:32) said the boy, "and I certainly think it is wise not to play with an adder."

"My fine fellow," said the crafty man, "it will give me great pleasure if you will only come and drink just one glass of the best wine with me."

"My Bible says, 'If sinners entice thee, consent thou not,' " (Prov. 1:10) was his reply.

This was a stunning blow to the tempter who returned to his pal. "Well, did you succeed?" asked his friend.

"Not at all. That youngster is so full of the Bible I can't do a thing with him!"

Billy Graham said, "I am convinced that one of the greatest things we can do is memorize Scripture. The Scriptures speak to us in those moments when we look to the Lord for sustenance and strength." Having verses at our memory tips will help us demolish the strongholds of evil.

A Personal Testimony

I made my decision for Christ during an evangelistic campaign led by Dr. Oscar Lowry, author of the book, *Scripture Memorizing for Successful Soul-Winning.* In this book he tells how he entered training for Christian service with an undisciplined mind. Because he felt he simply could not memorize Bible verses, he filled the flyleaf of his Bible with references helpful for counseling, which he then would have to look up when dealing with others. Though better than nothing, this did not satisfy him, so he determined to conquer his poor memory. "If I can memorize one verse," he said to himself, "then I can memorize one more, and ten more, and even one hundred."

Rising early the next morning he chose what seemed to him a difficult passage, Romans 10:9-10. He paced the room, saying to himself, "I will do this thing." He wrestled this way for half an hour until he had the passage completely mastered. Though to others this victory would seem minor, to him it was the beginning of better days.

The second morning he reviewed Romans 10:9-10, then memorized another verse. He kept adding a new verse each morning, and each day carefully reviewing those formerly memorized. Some months later it dawned on him that he could repeat one hundred verses without looking at the Bible. He also found the work becoming easier. And his heart was filled with joy as he had greater ease in witnessing and counseling. Before his death he had learned over 20,000 verses—about two-thirds of the Bible—and was able to locate each with chapter and verse.

As a new Christian fifteen years of age, I read Dr. Lowry's book and then began to memorize Bible verses. I made my own small verse cards. On one side I would write the reference and on the other side the verse. I would master the verse, and then review it every day for a week, at the same time learning another each day. When I mastered a verse thoroughly, I would put it in a pile to be reviewed weekly. Later I would place it in a pile for review once a month. I put the cards in packs of twenty. Finally, some packs would be reviewed only once every six months.

I picked what seemed significant verses, eighty from Matthew alone, so that three years later when I went to Moody Bible Institute, I could quote hundreds from memory with correct location. Probably no other factor contributed more to my spiritual growth than did this memorization. Decades later I still remember those verses.

Many individuals have memorized large portions of the Bible. As a boy C. H. Spurgeon memorized selected verses, partly because his grandmother saw its value and paid him cash to do so. John Ruskin memorized Psalm 119 (176 verses) because his mother required him to do it. Frances Ridley Havergal memorized the New Testament, the Books of Psalms and Isaiah in her teens. It is reported that some modern evangelists have memorized most, if not all, of the New Testament. Charles Lynch, self-made owner of a chain of Lucky Convenience Markets in the Baltimore area, was challenged when someone said, "Any stupid person can learn Scriptures." He thought, "I don't have any education so perhaps I could learn." He has memorized the Sermon on the Mount in Matthew 5—7, Romans 6—8, Galatians 5—6; 1 Corinthians 13; James 1 and 4, and many other portions.

Helps on Memorizing

Knowing the value of memorizing, the secular world has many

methods to suggest. Jerry Lucas, once star player for the New York Knicks basketball team and known for his prodigious memory feats, wrote *The Memory Book,* which contains a wealth of information on various memory systems. For example, early Greek and Roman orators, lacking handy note-making devices, linked each thought of a speech to a part of their homes. The opening thought would be linked to the front door, the second idea to the vestibule, the third to a piece of furniture in the vestibule, and so on. This is where we get the phrase, "In the first place."

Association is probably the best known technique. The lines on the music staff, EGBDF, are recalled by the sentence, *E*very *G*ood *B*oy *D*oes *F*ine. The four spaces are easily remembered by the word, *FACE.* Another suggested technique is to connect the word you wish to remember to an object that's ridiculous. Still another, to use substitute words like *mini soda* to recall *Minnesota.* Though these systems doubtless work for many, others find the effort more demanding than simple memorization.

• Remembering names. One of the sweetest sounds to a person is his name. If you are not interested enough in a person to learn his name, are you genuinely interested in his soul's welfare? The Lord Jesus "calleth His own sheep by name" (John 10:3). It is important to hear a new name clearly. If you don't hear it distinctly, don't let timidity keep you from asking the person to repeat it. To reinforce the mind, ask for the spelling. As soon as possible repeat the name in conversation, and when leaving, use it again. Later, jot it down in a notebook and go over it again, perhaps praying for that individual. On meeting him next time, call him by name.

You may wish to associate the name with something, but this carries risks. Dr. V. R. Edman, former president of Wheaton College and known for his ability to remember names, met a lady from his community at a Bible conference. She approached with the question, "Do you remember me?"

"Yes," he replied, "you're Mrs. Snow."

"No," she corrected him, "I'm Mrs. White."

Some keep lists of new names according to where they met the person: at work, school, church, Bible conference, or convention.

• Memorizing Scripture. Select your own verses. The more meaningful to you, the easier they are to memorize.

Use a wallet-size card system. Write the reference on one side, and the verse on the other. Do not leave a verse until you have thoroughly mastered it. Learn the reference first. Then add the first phrase. When this is mastered, add the second phrase, then the third and other phrases. It's better to progress slowly than to overload your mind with verses only partially learned. If you memorize two verses a week, you will know 100 in a year, and 1,000 in ten years.

Review every verse regularly. After you have said a verse correctly for several days, put it in a pile to review only once a week, then later in a pile for monthly review, and later go over it only once every six months. If you have a hard time with a verse, put it back in a pile for more frequent review.

Repeat the verse out loud. As we said before, *meditate* in one sense means "mutter." It is easier to memorize by muttering audibly.

Devote a definite time each day to memorizing. One of the beauties of the card system is that it can be used anytime or anywhere, workbench, desk, dresser, pocket, bulletin board, on bus, train, or plane.

Use memorized verses in your praying, letters, counseling, comforting, witnessing, meditating, and in fighting temptation.

Beware of rote learning—the ability to recite verses formally, but with little sensitivity or personal application. "This people draw near with their mouth and honor Me with their lips, while their hearts are far from Me, and their fear of Me is a commandment of men learned by rote" (Isa. 29:13, RSV).

On January 19, 1981 Chet Bitterman, a Wycliffe missionary about to begin language study with the Carijona Indians of Columbia, South America, was kidnapped by six terrorists. After forty-eight days of captivity, filled with threats, deadlines, and rumors, the missionary was shot by rebels who left his body in a hijacked bus.

During the months preceding his kidnapping, Bitterman had memorized all of First Peter. This book, written to encourage first-century believers in their fiery trials, gave him great strength in those difficult days. First Peter also told Chet how he should act toward his captors. In a letter to his wife, he quoted:

Always be prepared to give an answer to everyone who asks you to give the reason for the hope that you have. But do this with gentleness and respect, keeping a clear conscience, so that those who speak maliciously against your good behavior in Christ may be ashamed at their slander (3:15-16, NIV).

Little did Chet Bitterman know, when he memorized this epistle, how soon he would need it.

6
What Motivates You?

A basketball fan, walking a busy New York City street, recognized the retired star, Wilt Chamberlain, coming his way. Excitedly pointing to a twelve-foot ledge, the fan asked the tall athlete, "Can you jump up and touch it?"

Chamberlain replied, "I've forgotten how to jump. But if you throw a $100 bill up there, I'll remember real quick!"

We're not often that honest about our reasons for doing things. Sometimes our motives are complex and varied, making it difficult for us to sort out why we did something. Lurking deep in our inner sanctums are hidden buttons which, when touched, cause us to act in certain ways, perhaps gallantly, perhaps ignobly. A young lady, jilted by her boyfriend, dropped out of college, returned home, and refused to eat. Another young lady, suffering the same disappointment, without resentment applied to a mission board and went to serve in Africa.

The dictionary defines *motive* as "any internal force that causes a person to act in a certain way; that which goes on

inside a person to give direction to his behavior." It's motivation which makes a tenured college professor leave his teaching career with salary, pension plan, and fringe benefits, to
teach in a struggling mission school in Bangladesh that offers
no guaranteed income, retirement, or benefits.

Mixed Motives

Our motives aren't always what they seem to be. In his book,
The Presentation of Self in Everyday Life, Erving Goffman
illustrates ways in which we play dramatic roles to convince
people we have admirable traits which in reality we do not
possess. The bank teller, who becomes a leader in the Boy
Scouts to put up a good front while he is embezzling funds, is
acting from basically immoral motives. Peter exposed Simon
the sorcerer who wanted the power of the Holy Spirit for selfish
purposes (Acts 8:18-24). We may be guilty of mixed motives
because of self-deception, and may need the services of a godly
counselor to sort them out (Prov. 20:5).

Two teenagers set up telescopes at nearby spots in a beautiful area of the Shenandoah mountains. The first lad charged
a mere ten cents to look through his telescope. The second boy
charged nothing. A tourist, taking advantage of the free look,
was so overwhelmed that he handed the boy a quarter, asking,
"How can you afford not to charge?" Came the reply, "After
people see my breathtaking view, they usually give me far
more than a dime. So I make more money by offering my view
free."

Attendance at a church in New England began to increase
considerably on Sunday mornings. The pastor was elated—
until he learned that town gamblers were using the hymn
numbers posted at the front to play the numbers game.

On a snowy day when cars traveled with difficulty, a man
who had a passenger in the front stopped for a hitchhiker. After

the driver had let the hitchhiker out at his desired destination, he explained to his passenger that an extra person in the back seat made for more weight and helped over the icy roads. Mixed motives!

Fond parents stood by their little girl's bed as she recited her evening prayer, "Dear Lord, now I lay me down to sleep." At the end she improvised a little, "And dear Lord, please send the lovely snow to keep the sweet little flowers warm all winter." Jumping into bed, she smiled mischievously at her parents who were glowing with pride, "I sure fooled the Lord this time. I really want the snow so I can play with my new sled!"

Dr. Carl F. H. Henry in *Christian Personal Ethics* hypothesizes about a grocery clerk who always packs exactly five pounds of potatoes for customer convenience. If asked why, he might give one of several replies. He wishes to establish a reputation for integrity with his employer and thus secure his job. Or, he hopes to succeed in business because he believes honesty to be the best policy. Or, having cheated in the past, he is doing penance by rigorous honesty. Or, he intends to cheat in the future but first wishes to establish a good reputation. Or, he hopes to gain heaven by honesty. Or—and this is the motive most pleasing to God—out of gratitude for God's forgiveness through the Cross, he wishes to obey Him (Eerdmans, p. 532).

Why did you make that speech? Why did you accept the chairmanship of that committee? Why did you sing that solo? When you waited to let a car back out of a difficult spot, was it kindness or because you wanted the parking slot? I heard of two partners in a funeral home who purposely joined different churches so as to double their potential for prospects.

Though we cannot always see the motives behind another's action, or even fully understand our own drives, the Lord sees our deep-down motives. "Every way of a man is right in his own eyes, but the Lord pondereth the hearts" (Prov. 21:2). He knows whether our deeds are for His glory or for our aggran-dizement. He also knows the depth of our motivation in thirst-ing after Him. He said, "Ye shall seek Me, and find Me, when ye shall search for Me with all your heart" (Jer. 29:13).

Levels of Motivation

Psychologist Abraham Maslov based his well-known theory of motivation on a hierarchy of needs, arranged like steps on a staircase. The bottom rung represents man's basic animal-survival, physiological needs, such as food, sleep, oxygen, and thirst assuagement. Unless these needs are met, people will not respond to higher matters. A desperately hungry man in a rescue mission, or a thirsty man in the sub-Sahara, will not likely listen to a sermon until their physical needs have been satisfied.

When a person's physical needs are met, a second level of desires comes to the fore. This second step on the staircase is the need for safety, involving shelter, protection, economic stability, and emotional security. When self-preservation is threat-ened, a fearful lifestyle results.

When safety is assured, attention can rise to the third level of needs. The third step is the need to belong, to love, and be loved. Feelings of acceptance help us to reach out in affection and companionship.

For those transcending the first three levels, the fourth step is the need for esteem. The search for status, importance, approval, and the respect of others leads to self-respect, worth, adequacy, and even guidance in career choice. One Christian author admitted that what prompted him to write books was not the desire for food, job security, or acceptance by fellow authors, but the need for esteem as reviewers raved about his books or readers sounded their praises.

The fifth and top plateau is the need for self-actualization. This involves fulfilling the desires for self-expression, purpose in life, growth, creativity, realization of goals and of one's highest potential. In his 1970 revision of the hierarchy, Maslov included "the need to know and understand" and "aesthetic needs" as higher aspirations in the area of self-actualization.

The desires to live in a mansion, be rich, famous, powerful, or have fun are all located on the lower levels of Maslov's staircase. Working long hours, jogging five miles a day, and dieting, though noble in one sense, if done just to achieve success in life, do not spring from high motivation. However, it's possible for Christians to do everything to the glory of God. If a believer works hard to have more money to give to the Lord's work, and takes care of his body because it's the temple of the Holy Spirit, he has added a new dimension to his goals. Adding spiritual purpose to his lifestyle can sanctify motivation on every level.

Christian Incentives

To a handful of obscure disciples Jesus gave the seemingly impossible commission to carry the Gospel to the ends of the earth. Yet the insignificant were insuperable so that within three months after Christ's ascension, their number had increased to thousands. Within three years, their scattered converts had carried the Gospel to surrounding countries. And within three decades, their influence had spread through much of the Roman Empire, so that there were converts even in Nero's palace.

This same driving force propelled the Apostle Paul, one of the most motivated Christians of all centuries. Despite beatings, persecution, imprisonments, stonings, shipwrecks, weariness, pain, hunger, thirst, cold, and nakedness, Paul plodded on, always abounding in the work of the Lord. External motivations could never have sustained the drive necessary to overcome these obstacles.

The motivations that impelled Paul can also compel our energies into aggressive Christian dedication. Though there are more, three stand out: the condition of the lost, the prospect of accountability, and Christ's love for us.

• The condition of the lost. The world is full of trouble. Every day the media screams flood, famine, crime, revolution, and war. Jesus, moved with compassion, met the physical needs of man, healing every form of sickness and feeding the hungry. We should never become hardened to pictures of starving children and beleaguered refugees. We must share the concern which beats in the heart of God for the bodily suffering and material deprivation of mankind.

In addition, we must see beyond man's physical needs to his spiritual lostness. Paul remembered the poor and on one occasion spearheaded an offering from Gentile churches to hungry Jews in Judea. But he spent most of his time ministering to spiritual needs. This kind of balance is suggested in the motto of World Relief, "Food for the body, and food for the soul."

Paul labored under no false delusion as to man's precarious plight. He knew that men without Christ are without hope and without God (Eph. 2:12). He charted the awful depths of depravity to which the unregenerate heart could descend in its moral filth (Rom. 1:18-32). He fully recognized the terrible indictment under which lost mankind rested, and knew that the whole world was guilty and without excuse (Rom. 3:10-19). No one needed to convince him of the dreadful judgment awaiting unbelievers (Rev. 20:11-15). The urgency of his message spurred him to plead, "Now is the accepted time; behold, now is the day of salvation" (2 Cor. 6:2).

As widely as he traveled, Paul never bothered to describe in his letters the lovely scenery he must have enjoyed, nor did he ever mention any of the wonders of the world, though he must have seen the Colossus of Rhodes and the Parthenon of Athens. His interest concerned the inner needs of mankind. The cry for help from the man of Macedonia motivated Paul to carry the Gospel to the European continent (Acts 16:10). He knew he had the answer to that cry in a message which was the power of God unto salvation (Rom. 1:16). This Gospel could give pardon to the penitent, grace for every trial, victory over the ruinous effect of iniquity, and hope for the future.

We need to recapture the awful realization that people apart from Christ—despite healthy appearance, financial prosperity, and fashionable clothes—are guilty before God and doomed to eternal death. A subconscious universalism can cut the nerve of our motivation. Deep down we somehow feel that God will provide a way out for lost people and save them in the end. The Wheaton Congress on Missions declared:

> The repudiation of universalism obliges all evangelicals to preach the Gospel to all men before they die in their sins. To fail to do this is to accept in practice what we deny in principle.

Though the external punishment of the lost may be an unfathomable and perplexing doctrine, we must hold to it with broken heart and tear-filled eye. Otherwise we will undercut the nerve of evangelism.

If we saw a man overboard, would we not throw him a lifeline? If we observed a blind man stumbling near a precipice, would we not shout to warn him? A teenage girl mentioned to the visiting evangelist that none of her professing Christian family had ever witnessed to her, adding, "Do they really believe I'm lost?"

One who has a sure cure for a dread disease cannot remain silent. Paul knew the remedy for the baneful blight of sin, and could not hold his peace. We too should be motivated by a similar sense of obligation.

• The prospect of accountability. Some argue that to live the Christian life with the idea of reward is a selfish motive. However, Jesus did hold out the promise of dividends as a legitimate incentive, advising, "Lay up for yourselves treasures in heaven" (Matt. 6:20). Those who sacrifice property and loved ones for His sake receive a hundredfold more in this life, plus eternal life in the world to come (Matt. 19:29). Even a cup of cold water given in Jesus' name will not go unrewarded.

Paul lived with the prospect of the judgment of believers: "We must all appear before the Judgment Seat of Christ; that everyone may receive the things done in his body" (2 Cor. 5:10). Based on this awesome prospect, he was compelled to persuade men to a right relationship with the Lord, and to labor acceptably (vv. 9, 11). As he ran the Christian race, Paul looked toward the finish line and to the Judge, from whose hand he hoped to receive a victor's wreath and from whose lips he desired to hear the commendation, "Well done, thou good and faithful servant."

Five separate crowns are mentioned in the New Testament: the incorruptible crown for the disciplined runner (1 Cor. 9:25-27), the crown of rejoicing for the soul-winner (1 Thes. 2:19), the crown of righteousness for victorious runners (2 Tim. 4:7-8), the crown of life for faithfulness unto death (James 1:12; Rev. 2:10), and the crown of glory for exemplary conduct (1 Peter 5:3-4).

Paul realized that wasted time, unused talents, misspent money, an apathetic heart—deeds of wood, hay, and stubble—would issue in by-the-skin-of-the-teeth salvation (1 Cor. 3:15). A man in his fifties, dying of cancer, told his pastor, "I'm troubled. Not about my salvation, for I've trusted Christ. What bothers me is that ten years ago our Sunday School superintendent asked me to teach a class of high school boys and I refused. I was too busy climbing the ladder in my company. Had I taken the class, I would probably have influenced eighty high school boys for the Lord. But I haven't used my abilities in the Lord's service. That's what troubles me. I'm ashamed to meet my Saviour."

If the reality of the Judgment Seat of Christ could grip us, might it not lift the level of our dedication? Paul urged:

> Whatsoever ye do, do it heartily, as to the Lord, and not unto men; knowing that of the Lord ye shall receive the reward of the inheritance: for ye serve the Lord Christ. But he that doeth wrong shall receive for the wrong which he hath done; for there is no respect of persons (Col. 3:23-25).

Heartily is literally "from the heart." True incentive must come from within.

The prospect of reward is given for our encouragement. Must I go empty-handed, or will I enjoy an abundant entrance into His kingdom?

• Christ's love for us. Important as the first two motivations are, another force probably gave Paul more impetus than both of those combined. This third incentive became his one compelling, all-consuming motive.

Not my love for Christ, but His love for me should lead to ethical obedience. We do love Him, but He loves us much more. We love Him because He loved us first. Knowing too well the evil propensity of the human heart, Paul would never make anything as unstable as *his* love for Christ the propelling power of his life.

It was divine love that sought out Paul when he was an active enemy of the church, blasphemer, persecutor, even murderer of believers and, by his own admission, "the chief of sinners" (1 Tim. 1:15). Gratitude for such undeserved love moved Paul to full devotion. The love of Christ constrained Paul (2 Cor. 5:14), holding him to the one major task of proclaiming Christ by lip and by life. One version puts it, "For the love of Christ leaves us no choice" (NEB). He was a bondslave to his Master. The love of Christ so overmastered him that he continually lived for Christ's sake, suffered "in behalf of Christ," hazarded his life, and was ready to die for the name of the Lord Jesus Christ.

Paul asks the same dedication of us, beseeching us by the mercies of God to present our bodies as living sacrifices (Rom. 12:1). These mercies are recounted in the earlier chapters of Romans, mercies based on God's love and extended through the Son who shed His blood on the cross for our redemption. Our grateful recollection of such goodness should motivate us to offer ourselves for His service.

A proverb says, "Routine is a hard master; labors of love are light." Witness Jacob whose fourteen years of labor to win Rachel seemed but a few days, so great was his love for her (Gen. 29:20). A new convert wrote in his diary in appreciation of forgiveness, "Well do I remember how in the gladness of heart I poured out my soul before God . . . I besought Him to give me some work to do for Him as an outlet for my love and gratitude."

Compelled by love, Hudson Taylor went out to China. Amid tremendous difficulties and against high odds, he learned the language, acclimated himself to the cultural differences, won multitudes to Christ, and founded the China Inland Mission.

Another young man, C. T. Studd, sports star of England in both cricket and rowing, gave up a large fortune and carried the Gospel as a missionary to three continents, India, Africa, and China. Why such drive? He said simply, "If Jesus Christ be God, and died for me, then there is no sacrifice too great for me to make for Him."

David Livingstone, pioneer explorer and missionary, traveled 28,000 miles through uncharted African jungles, opening up the territory for the Gospel as well as vigorously opposing the wretched slave traffic. When a movie on his life was in process of filming, the producers confessed a problem. Though they could easily reproduce jungle scenes and wildlife, they were at a loss as to how to convey to the public the power that kept Livingstone in the heart of Africa in almost impossible conditions. The secret of his lifelong consecration was found in his diary entry on his second-to-last birthday. It read, "My Jesus, my King, my Life, my All, I again dedicate my whole self to Thee."

Sometimes communists and followers of strange cults put Christians to shame with their all-out passion for their cause. Since Jesus Christ left heaven to come to earth to redeem man, shouldn't we be willing to carry the Good News? Since Jesus surrendered the riches, honor, and comfort of heaven and suffered agony in our behalf, shouldn't we be willing to give up personal gain, fame, and convenience, and suffer for Him? Since Jesus did all this for us when He was under no obligation to do so, how compelling that we who are under gigantic debt to His love go into all the world with tidings of His forgiveness!

Christ's love says, "I went. You go. I left. You leave. I surrendered. You surrender. I gave. You give."

Dr. Eric Frykenberg, veteran missionary who spent half a century in India, could regale friends with incidents of his life on the field. One day someone asked, "Dr. Frykenberg, what was the most difficult problem you ever faced?" Without hesitation he answered, "It was when my heart would grow cold before God. When that happened, I knew I was too busy. I also knew it was time to get away. So I would take my Bible and go off into the hills alone. I'd open my Bible to Matthew 27, the story of the Crucifixion and I would wrap my arms around the Cross. And then I'd be ready to go back to work."

Church leaders everywhere ask, "How can we motivate our people to do God's work?" The answer is the same as Dr. Frykenberg's. If devotion has dwindled and our hearts are not warm, we'll never be able to proclaim and live God's Word until we get away and wrap our arms around the Cross. Then with our inner selves saturated with the love of Christ, we'll be ready to get back to work.

> Were the whole realm of nature mine,
> That were a present far too small,
> Love so amazing, so divine,
> Demands my soul, my life, my all.

7
The Voice of Conscience

Thirteen-year-old Andrew Flosdorf of Fonda, New York eliminated himself from the National Spelling Bee in June 1983 when he told judges he had misspelled *echolalia*. They had not caught his mistake. Explained Flosdorf, "I couldn't live with myself. I didn't want to feel like a slime."

Since 1811, people have been sending money to Washington, D.C. to absolve themselves of offenses against the government—such things as evading customs duty, underpaying income tax, using stamps a second time, or pilfering military material. Emotional but unsigned explanations and pleas for mercy often accompany the payments. The money is placed in the Federal Conscience Fund which now totals well over three million dollars.

What Is Conscience?

Conscience has been called God's watchdog, umpire, spy, window, lash, sword, and vice-regent. Philosopher Immanuel Kant was so impressed with conscience that he said he knew of nothing more awe-inspiring than the starry heaven above us and conscience within. He termed it a court within man's inner-most being.

Both the Latin, *conscientia,* and the Greek, *suneidesis,* for *conscience* are combinations of the two words *with* and *know,* literally "joint knowledge."

What are the two items sharing joint knowledge? First, the moral law of God is written on man's heart from the beginning. (See Rom. 1:18-20; Heb. 10:16.) Prohibitions against murder, adultery, stealing, and lying (four of the Ten Commandments) appear worldwide, though the specific definition of each may vary from culture to culture. Second, conscience bears witness to the fact that the Law is engraved in the heart. Paul wrote:

> For when the Gentiles, which have not the Law, do by nature the things contained in the Law, these, having not the Law, are a law unto themselves; which show the work of the Law written in their hearts, their conscience also bearing witness, and their thoughts the mean while accusing or else excusing one another (Rom. 2:14-15).

The three functions of conscience are to distinguish between right and wrong, to urge us to choose right and reject wrong, and to approve when we do right and condemn when we do wrong. Conscience has been called the ethical sense organ. It is not so much the voice of God in man but more accurately the voice of man in man. Conscience is man himself speaking as a moral being to himself, passing moral judgment on his own acts.

Nowhere is human life without this monitor, this second "I" which views our motives, words, and deeds objectively and then reaches a verdict. Planted ineradicably in man's being from the beginning, conscience provides strong evidence for the existence of a Supreme Moral Being. Man may rant and rave against God, ridicule His existence, and defy His authority. But the more he rebels, the more the inner voice hounds him for his folly and convicts him of his accountability. Light is given to every man who comes into the world, perhaps the final means by which God preserves a hold on man, calling him back from his wandering ways to the eternal home from which he has drifted (John 1:9).

Philosophers acknowledge the existence of conscience. Socrates called it *Daemon,* the intuitive monitor of ethical life with which man has always to contend in this moral universe. Aristotle said conscience differentiated man from beast. Aquinas defined conscience as "the mind of man passing moral judgment."

Though the word *conscience* itself does not appear in the Old Testament, it's writers knew the concept well. Conscience was evident at the beginning of biblical history in the shame and fear of Adam and Eve as they tried to hide from God. Cain's guilty conscience made him cry out, "Everyone that findeth me shall slay me (Gen. 4:14). David's "heart smote him after that he had numbered the people," and most vividly after his double sin of adultery and murder (2 Sam. 24:10; Ps. 32:1-5; 51:1-12). Likely the writer of Proverbs was referring to conscience when he spoke of the lamp of the Lord searching the spirit of man (20:27). Was not Isaiah alluding to a troubled conscience when he spoke of the wicked being like the restless sea whose waters relentlessly keep casting up mire and dirt? (57:20-21)

Though Jesus never used the precise word *conscience,* He affirmed its existence when He challenged the Pharisees to judge "what is right" (Luke 12:57). He had the pangs of conscience in mind when He told of a rich man in hell who was reminded how well he had fared on earth in contrast to a poor beggar.

The word *conscience* occurs thirty-two times in the New Testament, about two thirds of them in Paul's writings.

Since God created man as a moral being, in the image of God who is a Moral Being, God endowed man with this moral faculty. Because the natural law written on man's heart at the beginning has been distorted by the Fall, conscience is not an infallible guide. True guidance has been provided by the authoritative Scriptures.

Conscience Disturbs and Convicts

Every counselor sees people suffering pangs of conscience. Many hug to themselves their guilty secrets and memories of terrible deeds that keep inflicting wounds. Tennyson described censuring conscience as a "silent court of justice in his breast" and himself both judge and prisoner at the bar, ever condemned. Shakespeare had Richard III exclaim,

> "O coward conscience, how dost thou afflict me!
> My conscience hath a thousand several tongues,
> And every tongue brings in a several tale,
> And every tale condemns me for a villain"
> (King Richard III, iii).

Both the Old and New Testaments provide examples of stinging conscience. When Joseph revealed himself to his brothers in Egypt, they were troubled at his presence (Gen. 45:3). Earlier they had admitted, "We are verily guilty concerning our brother, in that we saw the anguish of his soul, when he besought us, and we would not hear; therefore is this distress come upon us" (42:21).

When Herod heard of a new popular teacher, his guilty conscience made him think it was John the Baptist—whom he had beheaded—risen from the dead (Matt. 14:1-2). Though wicked

Herod could silence the Baptist by a bloody ax, he could not silence his own inner voice.

A man driving a truck loaded with stolen coffee noticed a car bearing down on him from the rear. Imagining the car to be a police cruiser, he turned abruptly into the next driveway and crashed against a wall. The speeding car kept driving on. But other drivers, seeing the accident, phoned the state troopers who on investigation discovered the stolen merchandise and arrested the injured driver. Conscience makes "the wicked flee when no man pursueth" (Prov. 28:1). It is conscience that makes a lie detector work.

Conscience comes in lonely hours, awakens us in the night, stands by our beds, and makes us listen. One prisoner had nightmares in which the man he admitted murdering came back every night for years to sit on his bed and talk to him.

If we try to steel our conscience against some misdeed, the voice may then persist in our subconscious. A secretary affirmed that she had no regrets about an affair she was having with her boss. But as her "indiscretion" progressed, she became increasingly irritable and experienced pains which had no physical basis. Then she became depressed and, for the first time in her life, was unable to sleep. No matter how she tried to rationalize her conduct, she was still under the influence of the moral code in which she had been brought up. Her conscience was telling her she was violating this code. This resulted in physical discomfort, feelings of unworthiness, and a sense of guilt. "Be sure your sin will find you out" (Num. 32:23)—in your conscience.

Kinds of Conscience

• Evil conscience. The person who frequently violates his conscience will develop an evil conscience. It will become even easier to break God's Law. The student who cheats on an exam will find it less bothersome to his conscience the next time he cheats. With each advance of sin, conscience is further brutalized.

The conscience will soon proceed from preferring evil to delighting in it. Beyond simple disobedience, such people move to rebellion and ultimately to the degradation of those who "knowing the judgment of God, that they which commit such things are worthy of death, not only do the same, but have pleasure in them that do them" (Rom. 1:32).

An evil conscience is not beyond rescue. The accusers of the woman taken in adultery heard Jesus say, "He that is without sin among you, let him first cast a stone at her." They were "convicted by their own conscience" and all left (John 8:7, 9). The writer of Hebrews invited his readers to draw near to God "with a true heart in full assurance of faith, having our hearts sprinkled from an evil conscience" (10:22).

• Seared conscience. Every time we violate our conscience we become less sensitive. Conscience can become hardened like a callus on the foot. The car buzzer that indicates the safety belt is not on may startle us the first few times; but after some weeks of disregarding it, we never hear it. Paul warned Timothy of some who would depart the faith with "their conscience seared with a hot iron" (1 Tim. 4:1-2).

When the Bible speaks of stubbornness of heart, it means a hardened conscience. Pharaoh hardened his heart. Governor Felix trembled as Paul reasoned about the need for righteousness and judgment to come, but he did not respond to the Gospel in the two following years, and his conscience hardened. A little boy defined conscience as "that little three-cornered thing inside me which, when I do wrong, turns so much that the corners become worn and do not hurt me anymore."

We see a seared conscience in those depraved people who deliberately hook unsuspecting boys and girls on a drug habit, then grow rich in selling them drugs to maintain their vicious enslavement.

• Purged conscience. How may we rid ourselves of a nagging conscience? We can try to rationalize it, neutralize it, minimize it, revise it, or anesthetize it by drowning it out. But none of these will work. We need to face it and seek the remedy of divine purification through the Cross.

Conscience cannot be cleansed by Old Testament sacrifices or by moral reformation. What we need is to accept Christ as our Mediator, putting our faith in Him who made a once-for-all offering of Himself on the cross, and who is therefore able to purge our "conscience from dead works to serve the living God" (Heb. 9:9-14).

Millions have learned to live with their conscience by accepting God's pardon through Jesus who "cleanses us from all sin" (1 John 1:7). When conscience reminds the believer of a specific accusation of wrongdoing, he agrees with every charge, admitting, "I'm guilty." When conscience persists in its charge—"You know the wages of sin is death. God must punish you, so you're lost"—the believer replies, "That's where you're wrong. God in His mercy provided a substitute who took my guilt and paid my penalty. On the cross He suffered the pangs of hell for me. And when He rose from the grave the third day, He tore up the accusations against me, and promised I'd never have to appear in the court of heaven for any of my misdeeds. Accusing conscience, go away!"

A lady, whose sins of earlier years kept bothering her, sought the help of her pastor. She said she had asked the Lord dozens of times to forgive her. The pastor asked, "Do you believe He has?"

"Oh, yes," was her reply, "I believe the Lord has forgiven me, but how can I forgive myself?"

The wise pastor said slowly, "You must be holier than God."

The lady looked puzzled. The pastor explained, "Must God sacrifice another Son just for the sake of your conscience? If the death of Christ was good enough to satisfy God, isn't it good enough for you?"

After breaking down and weeping in relief, she said, "This is the first time in years that I feel no blame."

Untold millions rest in the promise, "There is therefore now no condemnation to them which are in Christ Jesus" (Rom. 8:1). They can say, "Now my conscience is at peace. From the law I stand acquitted."

• Good conscience. Defending himself before the Sanhedrin, Paul asserted, "Men and brethren, I have lived in all good conscience before God until this day" (Acts 23:1). On trial before Felix he claimed this as a goal, "Herein do I exercise myself, to have always a conscience void of offense toward God, and toward men" (Acts 24:16).

His good conscience was Paul's witness when he said he had great heaviness and continual sorrow in his heart for his unbelieving kinsmen (Rom. 9:1-2). He spoke often of his good conscience (2 Cor. 1:12).

To have a good conscience requires subjection to the law of the land (Rom. 13:5). Godly living must back up our orthodox beliefs if we would hold "the mystery of the faith in a pure conscience" (1 Tim. 3:9). Countering persecution with good behavior shames false accusers and gives the suffering believer a good conscience (1 Peter 3:16). John equated a good conscience with walking in the light; but he who hates his brother will not have a good conscience (1 John 1:7; 2:9-11). He also equated a good conscience with confidence in the prospect of Christ's return and of judgment (1 John 2:28; 3:19-21; 4:17-18).

A good conscience is sensitive, purified, and enlightened. Two proverbs declare, "No pillow is as soft as a clear conscience," and "A good conscience is a continual feast."

• Defiled conscience. The minute a person violates his con-science he has defiled it. The weak brother at Corinth, believing it wrong to eat meat previously offered to an idol, overrode his conviction and thus stained his conscience. If that inner voice is prodding you because of your excessive attachment to a sport, to your stereo collection, your boat, or your television set, don't stifle the voice.

• Weak conscience. Much meat in the Roman world was dedicated to idols in the temples before it was transferred to the markets for public sale. Some new converts insisted that Christians could have nothing to do with such meat. More mature believers did not see anything immoral in eating meat formerly dedicated in a temple, for they knew that an idol was nothing but a piece of carved wood or stone. Paul said that those who shrank from eating such meat possessed a weak and defiled conscience (1 Cor. 8:7).

The person who bends his conduct to a set of man-made, extrascriptural rules has a legalistic or weak conscience. If scrupulosity is carried to extremes, the result is a morbid, neurotic, rigid, unhealthy, oversensitive conscience.

Developing a Strong Conscience

How do you avoid a weak conscience and build a strong one? The following suggestions assume that you have initially purged your conscience through faith in the cleansing blood of Christ.

• Follow your conscience. Though conscience is not an infal-lible guide, and may be right or wrong, you should always obey it. To fail to follow your conscience is to do wrong. To act from conscience does not make an act right, but to act against conscience is wrong.

To follow the light that you have makes for the possibility of more light. But to take a step against conscience is to blur further enlightenment, and thus take a step on the road to disaster. Paul wrote, "Happy is he that condemneth not him-self in that thing which he alloweth. And he that doubteth is damned if he eat, because he eateth not of faith; for whatsoever is not of faith is sin" (Rom. 14:22-23). How often we have heard a preacher say, "If in doubt, don't!" A good conscience sets up a red flag when you contemplate a course of action you know to be contrary to the Word of God.

Conscience is a very delicate instrument. When it gets out of line, you're in trouble. The minute conscience is overridden, it is defiled and your fellowship with God is disrupted. Thomas Aquinas said that he would have to disobey the command of the superior he had vowed to obey, if that superior asked him to do anything against his conscience. To repeatedly trans-gress conscience endangers spiritual life, and may lead to spiri-tual shipwreck (1 Tim. 1:19).

• Restore a defiled conscience. As soon as you are aware of defiling your conscience, you should immediately confess your wrong to the Lord, thus securing His cleansing from the defile-ment. King David went too long, about a year, after his double sin of adultery and murder. He let inward groaning disturb his peace all that time (Ps. 32:3). Not until the Prophet Nathan confronted him did David cry out for mercy and find restored joy (Ps. 51).

Renewal of conscience may require restitution or action of some sort. Zaccheus made fourfold payment to those he had defrauded (Luke 19:8). The Ephesians, seized with fear over their secret practice of sorcery, brought their charms, worth thousands of dollars, and burnt them publicly (Acts 19:17-19). After a revival in a small town, the local doctor reported that hundreds of dollars of hopelessly bad debts were paid him by people who wished to wipe clean the slate of conscience. A remorseful robber who professed finding Christ repaid $3,300 stolen from a Denver bank two years earlier. He mailed a cashier's check drawn on a California bank under the alias, "R. E. Morse."

• Respect the conscience of others. Wide disagreements exist in various cultures over certain practices not specifically mentioned in the Bible. A southern believer, repelled by a mixed swimming party, may offend his northern brother by lighting up a cigarette. A European believer said to an American Christian visitor, "When I see the way you Americans injure your bodies by smoking, I could almost cry in my beer."

Those who hold broader views tend to be contemptuous of those whom they consider stick-in-the-mud reactionaries. And those with narrow outlooks easily criticize those who do things they think wrong. Paul rebuked both groups for their condemning attitudes. He commanded them not to judge one another in debatable matters but to respect each other's conscience. Since no two people require the same amount of food, what may be sufficient for one person may be gluttonous for another. We are to let others grow into Christlike maturity under their own responsibility, not laying down rules or expecting them to knuckle under our particular opinions. We must let each individual decide for himself the spiritual ramifications and consequences of any given deed.

• Realize your conscience is not an infallible guide. Though the precepts of morality were written on man's heart at the beginning, so that no one is devoid of moral sense, it does not follow that man possesses accurate ethical judgment. Because of neglect, environment, education, culture, or involvement in vice, wide disparity exists in the reactions of conscience to the varying standards of moral conduct. A Hindu once said to a British official, "Our conscience tells us it is right to burn our widows on the funeral pyres of their husbands." The official replied, "And our conscience tells us it is right to hang you if you do."

• Enlighten your conscience. Because of the radical range of influences on our early lives, consciences vary widely—from those who rarely feel guilty about anything to those who feel guilty about everything. If conscience is not an infallible guide to behavior, what then does constitute a Christian guide? A Christian conscience that is increasingly reliable is one that bears the impress of the Word of God. That conscience is educated in the written will of God.

Seventeenth-century divines, believing conscience was a special faculty placed in man for the purpose of judging moral actions, did not leave the education of conscience to chance. Holding that moral truths could be deduced from biblical premises, many of them wrote study manuals in which problems of conscience were organized into three major categories, those relating to God, to neighbor, and to self. Each category had several subdivisions, covering every area imaginable. In some instances, an author could indicate proper behavior because of direct commands in the Bible. In problems which did not permit clear-cut answers, the authors displayed impressive moral insight.

To develop a good conscience, you must acquire a clear knowledge of God's moral Law. This demands daily reading of God's Word and meditation on its precepts. Then you must practice lining up your conscience with biblical standards. Over and over you need to make proper choices until you develop the habit of following a conscience imprinted with the mind of God. Joseph was victorious in his skirmish with Potiphar's wife because he had made purity a habit of life through earlier years. His enlightened conscience would not let him sin against God.

It's not enough to say, "God is leading me," or "God is speaking to me," unless that guidance agrees with the written Word of God. A good rule is this: A voice never takes precedence over a verse. Any compulsion to run counter to the Word of God does not have its source in God. Because it is easy to confuse God's supposed voice with your own desires, you need the objective standard of morality found in the written Word of God.

When Martin Luther was summoned to the Diet of Worms to give account of his "heretical" writings, he made his famous statement, "My conscience is captive to the Word of God. I will not recant anything, for to go against conscience is neither honest nor safe. Here I stand, I cannot do otherwise. God help me. Amen" (Roland H. Bainton, *Here I Stand, A Life of Martin Luther,* A Mentor Book, p. 144).

A tormented conscience is a chamber of horrors. A cleansed conscience is a hallowed place, especially if that conscience is enjoying increasing enlightenment from the Word of God and practice in godly behavior.

8
Pruning Your Pride

Some car owners have phones in their cars to carry on business during the long drives to and from work. They get a kick out of closing a deal while waiting for a red light to change. However, many people want car phones just for the pride of phoning home, "Honey, I'm on the freeway. I'll be home in twenty minutes."

Not wishing to wait their turn on a long list, many try to secure this status symbol by pretending they are doctors, sneaking the phones back from distant cities, or by offering bribes. Others mount phony antennas on their cars. One company official estimated that there were as many car phonies in his area as car phones.

Kinds of Pride
Many are the types of pride: of place, face, race, lace, ace, even of grace. Caught up in the relentless pursuit of status and success, materially minded Americans lay great stress on such symbols as furs, clothes, jewels, mansions, big cars, and coun-

try club memberships. Often we spend money we don't have, to buy things we don't need, to impress people we don't like.

• Pride of appearance. An auto dealer noticed that sales skyrocketed after he installed mirrors over all his walls. This was because prospective buyers could see what they would look like to their neighbors as they drove down the street in their new cars. Millions are spent annually to make us look lovely, hair in style, skin smooth, shape trim, and appearance youthful.

A lady was resting comfortably in the recovery room after surgery. The doctor reported to her husband at the foot of the bed, "She's doing nicely. And besides, she's got age on her side." Then he added, "How old is your wife?" The husband answered quickly, "Forty-four." The wife, until then motionless, stirred slightly. Her lips formed a word. Husband and doctor both bent forward and caught her whisper, "Forty-three."

• Pride of achievement. A young man received a medal from an organization which used extravagant language to praise his accomplishments. Jubilantly, the prizewinner repeated the words at home to his mother. Then he asked, "Mother, how many great men are there in the world today?" His mother quietly answered, "One less than you think!"

It's possible for church members to be proud of the largest Sunday School, the biggest missionary budget, or the most spacious new sanctuary in their denomination. According to C. S. Lewis, pride is basically competitive. He suggests that we dislike the big noise at the party because we want to be the big noise.

Prune Your Pride

A restored monastery in Ephrata, Pennsylvania has low doorways and many folks accidentally bang their heads in passing from one room to another. The guide points out that the low openings were to teach humility. This architectural feature may jolt tall people to the need of lowliness, but how may the short, as well as the tall, learn humility?

• Realize that we all possess some pride. We don't have to be pretty, rich, or educated to be proud. A twelve-year-old girl, conscious of a scar on her face, found the answer to her problem by carrying an umbrella on both rainy and sunny days. A neighbor noticed that when she played games she tossed the umbrella on the ground, but picked it up on leaving. Taking her aside, the neighbor said, "You are a very conceited little girl." Taken aback, the little girl asked how that could be when she had such a scar. The neighbor countered, "Why do you always have that umbrella over your head when you leave for home? I want to ask you a favor. Tomorrow, leave the umbrella at home, and tell me if people look at you." The little girl tried it. As she began walking down the street, she pulled her head down into her coat; but sensing that no one was noticing her, she began to walk with head erect, and was released from the pride that had controlled her for so many weeks.

The poor can be proud. Socrates said to a man who purposefully wore torn clothes, "I can see your pride right through the holes in your cloak!" In Nebraska, twenty-six contestants vied for the honor of owning the rottenest sneakers.

The unschooled can be proud. People often hesitate to ask questions because in their pride they do not wish to reveal their ignorance. On a trip to Europe a handsome Algerian took sick and was hospitalized. He fell in love with his beautiful German nurse and they became engaged. He had to return to his homeland to straighten out his affairs before returning to Germany for the wedding. Though a series of love letters flowed from Germany to Algeria, the nurse received none in return. Finally, she wrote, "If you don't answer me, I'll kill myself." When no response came in the next few weeks, she poisoned herself. The news reached the Algerian as he was about to leave for a happy reunion with his intended bride. Asked by the puzzled police why he had not answered her letters, the brokenhearted Algerian admitted, "I cannot read or write. And I didn't want her to find out."

• Admit its subtlety. A Christian farmer, troubled by the sin of pride, walked early one morning to a little shed in a corner of his field. All day he prostrated himself on the ground before God. Walking home in the sunset, he thought, "Few men, if any, in this whole nation, have lain in the dust all day and become as humble as I am."

Pride is so subtle that we don't know we have it. Said one student, "I'm not proud, but with *my* brains I could be." We pray, "Lord, *keep* me humble," when we ought to pray, "Lord, *make* me humble." A young man received a medal for being the humblest employee in the company. But he wore it on his lapel and then wondered why they took it away from him.

Pride may unconsciously reveal itself in our frequent use of the first personal pronoun. A man authored a book *Humility and How I Attained It.* The printer ran out of I's as he was setting the type.

Pride shows up in the questions we ask. A little girl who had just won first diploma in her school class asked a pupil from another grade, "Who won first diploma in your class?" She asked this so she in turn would be asked who was the winner in her class, thus turning attention to herself.

Pride easily switches into mock humility, like Uriah Heap who said to David Copperfield, "I am the 'umblest person going." However Uriah Heap turned out to be not as humble as he claimed. A very competent artist often mentioned in private conversation, "I'm not a very good artist," hoping that others would contradict him and point out his abilities, thus catering to his pride.

Mock humility backs into our chitchat, as the ball player who disgustedly said, "I only hit three home runs today." Or the parent who lamented, "I wish my daughter would play more. She's always reading Plato and Hegel." Or the wife who remarked, "My husband always leaves me the Rolls Royce, and it's so hard to drive that big thing."

Pride is a vice from which no one is entirely free. While we hardly imagine we have it, it is quite visible to others, and possibly distasteful as well. Excessive self-esteem borders on self-worship, self-idolatry, self-deification. It was said of one well-known Christian leader, "He sometimes forgets that he's not God."

However, legitimate pride has its place. Perhaps the famous architect, Frank Lloyd Wright, displayed proper self-esteem when asked as a witness in a court of law, "Are you the greatest architect in the world?" Wright calmly replied, "Yes, I am." Later reprimanded by his wife, he protested, "But I was under oath to tell the truth!"

According to his autobiography, Benjamin Franklin drew up a list of virtues he meant to foster in order to cultivate his character. He set apart a certain period each day to practice each separate quality. He showed the list to a Quaker friend who, scanning the page, commented on the omission of the virtue of humility.

We often think of ourselves more highly than we ought. In fact, we can carry this interior pride right into church. Pride can march down the aisle and sit in a pew at 11 A.M. Sunday morning. Or it can perch on a soloist's or preacher's shoulder and whisper, "Boy, didn't I do well this morning!" People confess to a great many vices, but rarely does anyone confess, "My besetting sin is pride."

We need to acknowledge that we have it, but not like the salesman who said, "The trouble with our manager is that he won't admit his faults. Everyone ought to admit his faults. I would, if I had any."

• Remember that God hates and punishes pride. Pride defiles the inner sanctum: "Everyone that is proud in heart is an abomination to the Lord" (Prov. 16:5). The Lord hates a proud look (Prov. 6:16-17).

Moreover, the Lord exalts the humble, but casts down the proud (James 1:9-10). Satan wanted top spot in the universe, so God threw him down from his exalted position. Through pride Nebuchadnezzar was brought so low that he ate grass like the animals in the field (Dan. 4:30-33). Herod refused to give God glory and instead let people say of him, "It is the voice of a god." Immediately, God smote him dead (Acts 12:22-23).

Pride has its built-in hazards, as illustrated in the fable of the two ducks and the frog. These best of friends had to leave their home pond when it began to dry up. The ducks knew they could easily fly to another location. To transport their friend the frog, they decided to fly with a stick between their two bills, with the frog hanging on the stick with his mouth. A farmer, looking up from his field at the flying trio, remarked, "Well, isn't that a clever idea. I wonder who thought of that." The frog said, "I did." He learned the hard way that pride goeth before a fall.

• Recollect where you came from. An alcoholic walked into a Philadelphia rescue mission one bitter cold night with his torn sweater held at the neck with a safety pin. He had sold his overcoat to get a drink. That night he accepted Christ. On the second anniversary of his conversion, he visited the same mission and gave his testimony. Now well dressed, he told how the Lord had given him a good job. Then just before sitting down, he pulled from his pocket the safety pin which had kept his sweater shut the night of his conversion. He said that whenever he was tempted to think he was somebody, he would pull the pin out and look at it.

Gypsy Smith, famous evangelist of another generation, kept an old gypsy knife in a conspicuous place to remind him of the background from which God rescued him.

In a charitable institution in Munich, Germany, whenever a child was first admitted, someone took a picture of him in his ragged condition, just as he had been found begging on the street. Then he was bathed, fed, clothed, and educated. When he left years later, he was given the photograph so he wouldn't forget the deplorable life from which he had been snatched.

Bishop John Walker, the sensitive and caring bishop of the Episcopal Diocese of Washington, D.C., never forgot his humble upbringing in Georgia and Detroit. As chairman of the Black Student Fund he has helped to open up educational horizons for hundreds of disadvantaged youth.

We should never forget that before conversion, we walked according to the course of this world and our old nature, and were by nature the children of wrath. Then we should remember that God in His rich mercy gave us new life in Christ. Our pride will be diminished if we say with the psalmist, "He brought me up also out of an horrible pit, out of the miry clay, and set my feet upon a rock, and established my goings. And He hath put a new song in my mouth, even praise unto our God" (40:2-3).

• Reckon yourself dead. A seminary student came to the president's office to announce he was leaving school because fellow students were razzing him and making life unbearable. The president asked the young seminarian to hang his hat which he was holding. Looking all over the walls, the student protested that he could find nothing to hang his hat on. He was told to try to hang it anyway. When it fell to the ground, the young man exclaimed, "Sir, what do you mean by this?" Came the president's frank answer, "If the students could find nothing in you on which to hang their razzing, no evident vanity, they would leave you in peace." Pride had made him guilty of braggadocio and oversensitivity. He left the president's office with keener insight into his behavior.

Since our old natures have been crucified with Christ, we are to reckon ourselves dead to all that is wrong, pride, flattery, slights, and insults. Dr. R. A. Torrey came to a service to hear Dr. A. B. Simpson, founder of the Christian and Missionary Alliance. Simpson became so enthusiastic in his preaching that he forgot to acknowledge the presence of Dr. Torrey, an important evangelical figure of that day. So the next day he telegraphed Torrey his apology. Torrey wired back, "Dead—didn't even notice it." Andrew Murray said of humility:

> Humility is perfect quietness of heart . . . never to be fretted or vexed or irritated or sore or disappointed. It is to expect nothing, to wonder at nothing that is done to me, to feel nothing done against me. It is to be at rest when nobody praises me, and when I am blamed or despised. It is to be at peace as in a deep sea of calmness when all around and above is trouble.

• Ponder the frailty of the body. After permission was granted to move the graves of a cemetery that blocked a building expansion, one of the laborers dug up the remains of a coffin with a small metal plate, "Maud Prescott—Died 1912." Among the wooden remnants of the coffin the worker found a blackened skull, all that was left of Maud Prescott. He thought, "I wonder how old she was when she died. Did she have a nice house, wear pretty clothes, live a life pleasing to God?" Then he thought of what would remain of him sixty years after he was buried. It was humbling.

Though the bodies of believers will some day be glorified and perfect like Christ's resurrected body, the King James Version calls our present physical tabernacle "vile" (Phil. 3:21). Other versions call it "lowly, wretched, belonging to our humble state." We live in a body of humiliation because in its frailty the body can get so easily out of kilter, leaving us dizzy, para- lyzed, ulcerated, blind, deaf, feeble, immobile, or in agonizing pain.

We should not follow the example of St. Giles, patron saint of cripples and beggars, who reputedly refused to be cured of his lameness in order to more completely mortify his pride. Rather, we should take good care of our bodies as the temples of the Holy Spirit. Nevertheless, a visit to any nursing home will immediately remind us of the direction in which our bodies are relentlessly and irrevocably moving. Many recall the pa- thetic newspaper pictures of the late Dwight Eisenhower, the former commander in chief of Allied forces in World War II and President of the United States, who, in his declining years, was emaciated and feeble and confined to a wheelchair.

• Regard others as superior to yourself. When irritated by someone, we often say inwardly, "Who does he think he is?" But we really.mean, "Doesn't he know who I am?"

Much pride comes from an inflated view of ourselves along with a deflated view of others. We measure others in their bad moments and contemplate ourselves in our better times. Any dwarf, standing up, will find himself taller than a giant lying down. Instead of intoxication with our own achievements and good points, we ought to esteem others better than ourselves (Phil. 2:3).

The planner and builder of the tunnel under the Thames River testified he learned how to do it from a tiny shipworm. One day in visiting a shipyard he picked up a piece of lumber in which worms were at work. A proud man might have tossed the timber aside, "Get away, you little worm. I'm a master builder. You can't teach me anything." But he sat down and watched the worm at work, studying carefully the form of hole it was boring. Then the idea hit him as to how strong a tunnel would result if made in the shape of this hole. Later when asked to build a tunnel under the Thames, he undertook the assignment and succeeded.

John Owen, vice-chancellor of Oxford, would go to hear the unschooled John Bunyan preach whenever the latter came to London. When King Charles II expressed surprise that so learned a person would listen to so uneducated a person as Bunyan, Owen replied, "Had I the tinker's abilities, please your Majesty, I should gladly relinquish my learning."

• Remember the example of Jesus Christ. Ghandi, hero of India, though not a Christian, resisted the impulse to act arrogantly. This pruning of pride he learned partly from the New Testament. Convinced that servant-humility was a posture required by God, he threw away many material things, stopped wearing his European clothes, and sought friendship with the poor and afflicted. He did not permit any VIP to interrupt his lifestyle. When Lord Mountbatten offered to fly him to an important meeting in his private plane, Ghandi chose instead his usual third-class train compartment. Londoners gasped when they saw him walk down the gangplank wearing only a cotton loincloth and leading a goat (his source of milk) by a rope. Reporters were offended that he would dare meet with the King of England so scantily dressed. He refused offers from the finest hotels and stayed in an East End London slum.

No one exemplified the subjugation of pride more than the Lord Jesus Christ. His self-emptying is outlined in the well-known Philippian kenotic passage (2:5-8).

Though God, He became man.

Though resident of heavenly mansions, He came to this planet where he had no place to lay His head.

Though rich, He became poor.

Though Lord of glory and Creator of the universe, He walked around this earth unknown, unhonored, of no reputation, and rejected.

Though holy and righteous, He submitted to the kind of death reserved for aliens, slaves, and criminals.

With this model in mind Paul said, "Let this mind be in you, which was also in Christ Jesus." Therefore we are to "let nothing be done through strife or vainglory" (Phil. 2:5, 3). To find the sweet, elusive grace of humility we must take long and repeated looks at Him who said, "I am meek and lowly in heart" (Matt. 11:29).

• Reflect on the cross of Christ. By contemplating the cross of Christ we are confronted with the nastiness of our own personal sins which caused His sacrifice. If Jesus Christ had to die that shameful, painful death to rescue us, how sinful we must have been. This reminder should provide the deathblow to any pride of self-righteousness. Apart from Him we are helpless and can come to Him only as beggars. Our faith must rest in no merit of ours, but in the matchless, undeserved favor of Christ.

A proud society lady, deeply convicted of her sins, sought out a minister. Seeing she was very self-righteous, he repeated the words of Jesus, "Except ye be converted, and become as little children, ye shall not enter into the kingdom of heaven" (Matt. 18:3). Before long the lady began to break down in tears and repeat the same text. With pride stifled and face toward heaven, she came as a little child to ask mercy of Christ. She rose from her knees peaceful, pardoned, and joyful. She became firm in her convictions, and witnessed to her friends, many of whom were proud of spirit.

A proud heart is a chamber of abominations, but a broken and contrite spirit helps to create a holy heart. The hymnwriter said it well:

When I survey the wondrous cross,
On which the Prince of Glory died,
My richest gain I count but loss,
And pour contempt on all my pride.

9
Cultivating
Calmness

On the morning of his history exam; Junior awakes with a stomachache. Is it the flu or appendicitis or too much cake from last night's supper? His mother diagnoses his trouble as pressure from the test scheduled for that day.

Pressures pile up in our busy, hectic lifestyles—school stress, marriage problems, social pressures. Even missionaries suffer stress through cross-cultural change. No one is exempt from anxiety. Suicide is a leading cause of death among youth.

Psychologists have devised a scale of points for forty-three various types of stress, beginning with a value of 100 for death of a spouse and 73 for divorce, ranging down to 20 for a change in residence, 13 for going on vacation, and 11 for minor violations of the law. A score of 150 indicates minimal stress in one's life. From 150-350 turns on a caution light, warning of a 66 percent chance of illness within the next two years. Anything over 350 points is too much stress and indicates the person's need to gain control over his critical situations.

Persistent stress can precipitate a more debilitating state

known as burnout. Especially prone to this condition are people who need to succeed—the highly competent and the over-
committed. Like the engine that has almost used up its fuel,
the burnout victim suffers physical symptoms like headaches,
gastrointestinal problems, chronic fatigue, insomnia, hyperten-
sion, chest pains, loss of interest in work and home, irritability,
listlessness, rigidity, even hostility, and is unable to cope effectively. Perhaps the psalmist felt like this when he lamented,
"Therefore is my spirit overwhelmed within me; my heart
within me is desolate" (143:4).

A *New York Times* article pointed out that people who seem
outwardly calm in stressful situations may undergo hidden and
chaotic changes in their cardiovascular systems. This explains
why an executive who seems to take heavy work demands in
stride may suffer a fatal seizure. Though outwardly cool, inwardly he is a "hot reactor." The heart, pumping against
strong resistance, is like a car driven at top speed with its
brakes on ("Heart Attacks: Turmoil Beneath the Calm,"
20 June 1983).

In contrast to people hiding a seething heart, the Apostle
Paul had a peaceful interior despite a rough environment. He
wrote, "We are troubled on every side, yet not distressed; we
are perplexed, but not in despair" (2 Cor. 4:8).

How can we, like Paul, cultivate calmness within? How can
we survive the rat race so that our inner sanctum is not a
chamber of agitation and anxiety, but a place of holy tranquility? Here are some principles.

Realize Life Will Have Some Stress
Just as most plane flights have a few rough spots along the
way, so most life trips are not perpetually smooth rides but
bring their pockets of turbulence. Life has its thorns as well as
its roses. We cannot escape all unpleasant circumstances. In
fact, some stress is necessary for success in life.

A stranger accosted a New York City pastor on the street, and asked, "Can you tell me a place where I can find perfect peace?" The minister pointed to a park across the street over which an entrance sign read, "Sacred Heart Cemetery." He said, "In there are 5,000 people in peace." As long as we are alive we will have problems. No one can avoid tension and unpleasant situations. General Eisenhower said he had butterflies in his stomach on D-Day as his troops embarked on the invasion of Europe.

We cannot win every contest we enter or every game we play. Some of our brilliant suggestions will be vetoed, if not laughed at. Some of our motions will be voted down, or maybe not even seconded. We are bound to stub our toes on rocky paths along the way. Annie Johnson Flint put it, "God hath not promised skies always blue."

Confidence in the overriding providence of a loving, wise God will help us adjust to inevitable difficulties. We need to rest in the promise of Romans 8:28 that *all* things work together for good to those who love and belong to the Lord.

Rid Your Heart of Malice

No heart will enjoy calm if it is disturbed by hate, envy, simmering anger, resentfulness, or an unforgiving spirit.

Envy replaces joy with inner rankling when others get a job, or a promotion, or a new car, or some award. A little lad who had harassed his parents for months for a bike received one for Christmas, but was happy for just an hour. Riding off joyously to show his friend, he returned crestfallen, "Bob got a bike too. But it's bigger than mine!"

A pamphlet issued by the New York State Mental Health Department devoted a page to "Envious Ella," a housewife perennially dissatisfied over the superiority of her neighbor's possessions. Says the pamphlet, "Envy doesn't get fur coats, new cars, and round-the-world trips. It brings only misery. Life is hers to enjoy if she will stop letting envy gnaw at her nerves until they scream like a tormented cat." One Old Testament word for *envy* is from the root *to burn*. The Arabic word gives the idea of *raging fire*. Says Proverbs, "A sound heart is the life of the flesh; but envy the rottenness of the bones" (14:30).

How many times a day do you let yourself get irked? How easily does irritation lead to anger, and perhaps to a blow-up? An explosion is not the best reaction. On the other hand, stifling your aggravation, clamming up and harboring resent-ment, will only tear down your inner calm. Holding grudges and hurt feelings carry high price tags. Such moods often backfire, causing indigestion, stomach upsets, fatigue, insomnia, and even ulcers. One doctor said that many people suffer from "grudgitis." Often people say from between clenched teeth, "I'll get even if it's the last thing I ever do!" And sometimes it is the last thing they ever do! Another doctor commented, "What we eat may not harm us as much as what may be eating us."

Instead of letting resentment get deeply embedded in your craw, you should go to any brother with whom you are at odds, seek to be reconciled, and endeavor to rebuild the relationship. You should be always willing to react to others in a humble, loving, forgiving, and unselfish way.

Find Your Niche

Dr. O. Quentin Hyder, New York City psychiatrist, says every Christian should "develop for himself a place in life wherein he can feel secure and function successfully within the limits of his abilities" (*The Christian's Handbook of Psychiatry,* Revell, p. 51).

Every believer possesses talents and spiritual abilities as a gifted child of God. Thus, no Christian should have the disrupting influence of an inferiority complex. No false humility should make him moan, "I'm a nobody," or lead to burial of his gifts. Rather, awareness of his gifts should help meet his psychological need to feel wanted, and so contribute to his sense of inner well-being.

We should work within the context of our God-given strengths. A person becomes uncomfortable inside when he is not doing what he is best suited for. Hans Selye, leading authority in the field of stress, says that we should seek our own stress level. Some people are racehorses, while others are tortoises. If we try hard enough, we can always find a Beethoven or an Einstein with whom to contrast ourselves, and then bemoan our poor showing and feel woefully inadequate. An eagle should not be expected to be a good swimmer, nor should a rabbit accept an assignment to fly.

We should not normally push ourselves beyond our limits. The slaving Israelites in Egypt, commanded to make the same number of bricks as before but without straw, groaned under this extra burden. No one should voluntarily take on too many jobs or excessive responsibility. Some people can't say no and so they enroll in too many classes and serve on too many committees. They wrongly equate fidelity with fatigue, and end up in inward turbulence as they are pulled in every direction, not doing any job well. The early apostles said no to waiting on tables, for they had their tasks already cut out for them to do—the ministry of the Word and prayer (Acts 6:1-2). Awareness that we are doing what God wants us to do with the abilities He has given us provides our basis for healthy self-affirmation.

Why do people put unreasonable demands on themselves? Sometimes it's compulsion to compensate for a deeply felt inadequacy. Or maybe it's parental pressure. A doctor who really wanted to be a musician, but who gave in to his parents' expectations, may succumb more easily to the stress of his medical practice. Jesus did not heal everyone in Judea, Galilee, and Samaria, nor can we bear the burdens of the whole world.

If we would beat the rat race, we should find a niche where we feel at home and can produce effectively within the framework of our strengths. Life is a matter of choices. We need to bring our priorities under the will of God and try to do only what He wishes us to do, even rejecting good things in order to do the best.

Have Goals

Always have before you some goal which you are striving to achieve. When you reach that goal, then set another and go for it.

Some goals go with the various stages of life. The one-year-old is fulfilled as he learns to walk. The two-year-old derives satisfaction from shouting, "No." The ten-year-old is happy as he hits a home run in Little League, the high school senior as she gets a date for the big party. In young adulthood, goals may be college graduation, marriage, employment in one's chosen field, and parenthood, all of which, when successfully reached, give a sense of achievement. In his old age, Joshua was reminded by the Lord, "There remaineth yet very much land to be possessed" (Josh. 13:1).

If one has no purpose, then life lacks meaning and significance. A major reason for suicide is boredom—no reason for living. Americans have the highest rate of boredom per capita, so they turn to drink, gambling, entertainment, drugs, anything for a kick. But kicks wear off. People get fed up with life.

We all need goals, not just general "to glorify God" aims, but goals that are specific, few in number, attainable, and measurable. One Christian sets a maximum of four, one for each major area of life: physical, intellectual, social (family), and spiritual. One New Year's Day he had these resolutions:

- to lose twelve pounds during the year, one a month;
- to read at least one book a week;
- to give his wife an evening out a week, including a modest meal and enjoyment of each other's company;
- to memorize one verse of Scripture every week.

Even when we feel mired in some unfortunate situation, whether stemming from an unhappy childhood or a deprived environment, we should believe that things can be different through God's grace. People who have thought change impossible have been known to challenge their inferiority feelings, set goals beyond what they thought possible, and become the men and women God wanted them to be. In so doing, they have experienced the unimaginable delight of fulfillment.

In his book, *Anatomy of Illness,* Norman Cousins tells of meeting Pablo Casals, the noted cellist, for the first time just before the musician's ninetieth birthday. In his daily routine Casals would shuffle into the living room on his wife's arm, badly stooped, with his breathing labored from emphysema, head pitched forward, hands swollen, fingers clenched with arthritis. Before breakfast he would go to the piano bench, and with evident effort would raise his swollen and clenched fingers above the keyboard. Amazingly, his fingers would slowly unlock, his back straighten, his breathing ease. Then his fingers reached the keys. Soon he was playing a Brahms concerto, with fingers agile and powerful, racing across the keyboard with dazzling dexterity. His body was no longer shrunken but supple and released from arthritic restrictions. Later in the day he played his cello with fingers, hands, and arms in lovely coordination as they produced beauty of movement and tone. Cousins commented that he had seen a miracle. A man gripped with infirmities of age somehow cast off his affliction, even temporarily, because he had something of consuming importance to do. His desire to accomplish a specific goal issued in evident physical and psychological effects.

Take Time to Relax

Relaxation is essential for maintaining inward health and peace. Job burnout has been definitely linked to lack of vacation time in our society. All work and no play makes Jack a dull boy. Jesus told His disciples to come apart and rest awhile (Mark 6:31). Some deem it sinful to enjoy themselves; yet in dozens of wholesome pastimes, a Christian can have relaxing pleasure without guilt feelings that he is incurring divine disapproval. Jesus attended more feasts than fasts. Fun time is not wasted time; rather it is an economy that helps us recoup inner calm.

Recreation in this tense world is not a luxury but a must. On the average, Europeans have longer vacations than Americans, considering them an integral part of the work world. In France, yearly vacations total almost six weeks for nearly all employees. Month-long holidays are a tradition in Britain, Italy, Scandinavia, and Spain.

We should be able to look forward every day to some definite time or event which will be a change of pace from the day's work, whether it's a dinner engagement, a visit to a friend's home, working on a hobby, playing a game, physical exercise in a sport, gardening, or reading a few chapters from an interesting book. Likewise, we should look forward to some weekly recreation and to the Lord's Day with its rest and worship. And quarterly, we should take a long weekend, and annually, a vacation away from our regular routine.

Life is grim and serious enough as it is, so why not note the humor along the way? Your body won't let you laugh and develop an ulcer at the same time. Having a friend to listen to your frustrations will lessen inner turbulence. Psychiatrist

Walter Menninger of Topeka's famed Menninger Clinic says that after an exhausting day he finds choir practice quite therapeutic. He claims that if its healing quality could be bottled, it would outsell the tranquilizers.

Exercise has been called nature's tranquilizer. Thirty-minute periods of vigorous exercise release into the brain the same chemical found in antidepressants. One psychiatrist commented that he had never treated a faithful jogger for depression.

Nature teaches the importance of rejuvenation. We must take time for rest, rehabilitation, and recreation if we would maintain our inner equilibrium.

Strong Personal Trust in the Lord

Faith in Christ takes care of our *past*. Assurance of sins obliterated through Christ's death on the cross gives us a clean conscience. Faith in Christ also takes care of our *future*. Is He not named Prince of Peace? Some day He will bring peace to this tortured world. In the meantime, if death be our lot, we shall depart to be with Him who is the resurrection and the life. Trust in Christ also gives confidence in the *present*. In the Sermon on the Mount the Lord gave several short, sharp arguments to cure anxious, divided minds.

If God provides us the great gift of life, will He not also give us food to sustain it? If He gives us the gift of a body, will he not provide clothing to cover it? If God feeds the birds, who do not sow, reap, gather into barns, or catch buses, punch time clocks, or earn wages, will He not take care of us, even in old age? Martin Luther, seeing a bird sing and then tuck its head under its wing, commented:

This little bird has had its supper and is getting ready to go to sleep, quite content, never troubling itself as to what its food will be or where it will lodge on the morrow. Like David, it abides under the shadow of the Almighty. It sits on a little twig content, and let's God care.

Strong trust in the Lord makes for a contented, joyful, cheerful heart. Because of unbelief, repeated griping was characteristic of the Israelites. From their deliverance from Egypt to the conquest of the Promised Land, there was a constant undertone of murmuring. When the Egyptians pursued, the Israelites forgot God could deliver them. Shortly after their escape through the Red Sea, they longed for Egypt because they had no food or water. They had already forgotten that He who parted the Red Sea could easily provide manna and water. Later, they again complained of lack of water, so soon forgetting God's previous manifestations of power. Murmurings stem from short memories which forget to count blessings.

David's heart was disturbed many times by adverse circumstances. Often he said to his inner sanctum, "Why art thou cast down, O my soul? and why art thou disquieted within me?" Then he answered himself, "Hope thou in God; for I shall yet praise Him, who is the health of my countenance, and my God" (Ps. 42:11). Time and time again in deep distress, "David encouraged himself in the Lord his God" (1 Sam. 30:6).

Dr. Richard Chase, president of Wheaton College, said that when problems press in on him, causing him stress, he goes to the Scriptures and finds respite from pressures as his mind is turned toward the Lord. The Prophet Isaiah promised, "Thou wilt keep him in perfect peace, whose mind is stayed on Thee, because he trusteth in Thee. Trust ye in the Lord forever: for in the Lord Jehovah is everlasting strength" (26:3-4). Other passages that bring comfort include Deuteronomy 33:27; Psalm 23:1; Matthew 6:34; Romans 8:28, 31-39; Philippians 4:13.

Peter knew the secret of inner calm. The very night before

his scheduled execution, though the church was awake in an all-night prayer meeting, he slept so soundly that he had to be awakened by angelic blows (Acts 12:7).

Paul had the formula for inward peace. To paraphrase his own words in Philippians 4:6, it was, "Be anxious for nothing. Be prayerful for everything. Be thankful in anything." Verse 7 states the result, "And the peace of God, which passeth all understanding, shall keep your hearts and minds through Christ Jesus." Or restated, "The peace of God will garrison or protect your inner man."

Because Paul had learned the lesson of contentment, he and Silas could sing praises to God at midnight, though their backs were bloodied and bruised from a cruel beating. After a two-week raging storm at sea in which all hope of survival was gone, Paul could take the moral ascendancy and declare to all on board:

> "Be of good cheer: for there shall be no loss of any man's life among you, but of the ship. For there stood by me this night the angel of God, whose I am, and whom I serve, saying, 'Fear not, Paul; thou must be brought before Caesar; and, lo, God hath given thee all them that sail with thee.' Wherefore, sirs, be of good cheer: for I believe God, that it shall be even as it was told me" (Acts 27:22-25).

Paul could be content in whatever state he found himself, even when confined to a Roman prison where he made that seemingly impossible situation count for the progress of the Gospel (Phil. 1:12).

Christians are to be a joyful people, "teaching and admonishing one another in psalms and hymns and spiritual songs, singing with grace in your hearts to the Lord" (Col. 3:16). Proverbs says that "a merry heart doeth good like a medicine"

(17:22). In fact, "He that is of a merry heart hath a continual feast" (15:15).

Strong personal trust in the Lord needs practical outlets. As we help our neighbors, we discover that life counts. This sense of meaning adds to our inner peace. Helping push a neighbor's stalled car, or taking time to visit a sick friend, are good works that indicate to a believer that God is at work in his life. A sense of satisfaction comes through the confirmation that "we are His workmanship, created in Christ Jesus unto good works, which God hath before ordained that we should walk in them" (Eph. 2:10).

A missionary, living among the tribespeople of Colombia, South America, received in his monthly mail a computerized form letter from the alumni association of his alma mater, one of America's great universities. A cover letter said that his answers would be of great value in determining the success of the university's distinguished alumni.

The first question was, "Do you own your own home?" The missionary looked up at the palm-thatched roof which provided adequate shelter in the Amazon Basin. He had paid the tribesmen $125 for building it, so answered *yes*.

The second question was, "Do you own two homes?" Thinking of the heavenly home the Lord had promised him, he answered *yes*.

The third question was, "Do you rent quarters elsewhere?" Remembering the group house in Bogota where his family occasionally stayed, though it meant squeezing into close quarters with other colleagues, and sharing the same bathroom, again he answered *yes*.

The fourth question was, "Do you own a boat?" Again he answered *yes*, because tied up at the river bank below his house was a dugout canoe given him by the tribespeople.

"Do you plan to travel abroad for vacation purposes during

the next two years?'' was question five. Since furlough was due the next year, he said *yes.*

The sixth question asked the range of his income. Categories ranged from over $100,000 to under $10,000. He checked the latter.

The final question was, "How many automobiles do you own?" Since the river was his highway, and he had no use for automobiles, he filled in *none.*

A computer-programmer friend later told the missionary that his information was probably rejected by the computer with a notation, "Data incompatible." But the experience of filling out the questionnaire confirmed for him the words of Paul, "Godliness with contentment is great gain" (1 Tim. 6:6).

10
Controlling Your Self

A man walked to a newsstand to buy a paper. He thanked the proprietor politely, but the proprietor didn't even acknowledge his greeting. A friend observed, "He's a sullen fellow." The first man replied, "Oh, he's that way every night." His amazed friend asked, "Then why do you continue to be so polite to him?" Answered the man, "Why not? Why should I let *him* decide how *I* am going to act?"

Rather than let others control us, we should exercise self-control.

What Is Self-Control?

Self-control is last in the list of the fruit of the Spirit (Gal. 5:23) and is translated "temperance" in the *King James Version*. The Greek word is composed of two words, *in* and *strength,* so self-control literally means "within strength" or "inside strength" or "self-power." Many versions translate it "self-control." This trait which Paul repeatedly required in saints is rendered "self-controlled" by the NIV (Titus 1:8; 2:2, 5-6, 12). Peter likewise

115

commanded this quality, "Be clear minded and self-controlled" (1 Peter 4:7, NIV). He listed self-control among the virtues which we are to cultivate (2 Peter 1:6).

The Gospel was designed to take the policeman off the street corner and place him in our hearts. To live in our world without the police would be unsafe. But if within our hearts we have a dynamic whose authority we obey, we won't need a policeman outside us. This inside dynamic has been supplied as a fruit of the Spirit. God promised that by His Spirit the laws written on stone would instead be written within our hearts and minds (Jer. 31:33-34; Heb. 10:16). The Spirit gives us inner strength, self-control.

This within-power does not come from any human being, not even a spouse. When Mary's husband up and left her, she was devastated. She began to neglect her personal appearance. Blaming his absence, she moaned, "There's no one else on whom I so depend." Though some security does come from a good marriage, our basic relationship must be to the Lord Himself, the only independent and unchangeable One in the universe.

Too many people depend on money for security. "The rich man's wealth is his strong city" (Prov. 10:15). Or it may be fame, education, pleasure, personal appearance, or drugs. Waiting for a plane to take off one night after a delay, I heard a man exclaim, "I'm not going on that flight unless I get a couple of drinks first!"

Others rely on external authorities. The undisciplined practice their music for the teacher, run five miles a day for the coach, do the job on time so as not to irritate the boss. But the self-disciplined are self-sufficient, not easily rattled, possessing internal peace that enables them to think calmly, weigh the alternatives, and bridle their tongues.

Many housing areas today are self-contained, making it unnecessary for residents to go outside the complex. Within their grounds are all the essential services like grocery store, beauty shop, barber shop, bank, cleaner, clothing store, and post office. Such complexes resemble the person whose resources are all contained within, and who does not need to depend on anything outside. Incidentally, the word *content* is related etymologically to the word *contained.* The contented person, one who has inner strength, is self-sufficient, not relying on substitutes, is thus self-contained. Paul possessed this inner dynamic which enabled him to say, "I have learned, in whatsoever state I am, therewith to be content. I know both how to be abased, and I know how to abound" (Phil. 4:11-12).

Areas Where Self-Control Is Needed

• Alcohol. Alcoholism's toll is staggering, including untold wrecked lives and homes, millions of dollars lost in absenteeism and 30,000 deaths annually in the U.S. because of drinking drivers.

The Bible says we are not to be addicted to wine. Not only does intoxication show lack of self-control, but it leads to more loss of self-control. It stupefies, removes inhibitions, and makes us do things we wouldn't normally do. "Wine is a mocker, strong drink is raging, and whosoever is deceived thereby is not wise" (Prov. 20:1).

• Sex. Many Old Testament characters lacked self-control in the area of sex. Whenever Samson saw a girl he wanted, he asked his parents to get her for him, or just went and took her himself. David stole another man's wife. It is not surprising that David's son, Ammon, vexed with lust for his half-sister, Tamar, didn't possess enough inner strength to overcome his passion.

The first appearance of the word *self-control* (temperance) in the New Testament occurs in the story of Paul's reasoning with Felix in the matters of righteousness, self-control, and the judgment to come (Acts 24:25, NIV). According to the historian Tacitus, Felix revelled in lust, and began his career as a Roman procurator of Judea by seducing and marrying Drusilla, queen of a small Syrian state. Felix lacked mastery of self.

• Food. When we think of temperance, we immediately think of alcohol. We conveniently forget that gluttony is condemned in the Bible.

Hungry Esau sold his birthright for a mess of pottage. Eli's gluttonous sons grabbed animal sacrifices from the people in the temple even before they had been properly offered.

But Daniel purposed in his heart not to defile himself with forbidden meat and wine, and became better nourished on a simple fare (Dan. 1:8). What inner strength Jesus possessed! In great hunger after His forty-day fast, He refused to turn stones into bread, though He certainly had the power.

Bulging waistlines reveal that Americans have been caught in the food trap. Overeating is one of the most widely practiced and generally accepted sins in America. Those who are substantially overweight need this Christian virtue of self-control.

• Amusements. Granted, we all need a certain amount of relaxation, vacation, and hobbies. But if we let softness, luxury, TV, or worldly amusements shove the Lord's house and business to the background of life, we have become lovers of pleasure more than lovers of God.

Many make sports their god. A civic leader in Green Bay, Wisconsin said that everybody's schedule in that city is determined by the playing schedule of the Green Bay Packers. He added that while empty pews might dot the city's lovely churches, no empty seats would be found in their football stadium.

• Speech. No more accurate test of Christian profession exists than the ability to control one's tongue. Untamable by man, the tongue "is an unruly evil, full of deadly poison"

(James 3:8). Words can break up families, split churches, divide nations and, like a spark, can start a huge conflagration. A woman known for her violent temper defended her frequent outbursts, "They're always over in a minute." A fellow believer would not let her get away with that excuse, replying, "So is a shotgun blast, but it blows everything to smithereens!"

When tempted to give an unkind response, our inner strength should enable us to delay long enough to assess the situation and redirect our irritation into a proper and constructive direction. Self-control permits the soft answer that turns away wrath (Prov. 15:1). "He that is slow to anger is better than the mighty; and he that ruleth his spirit than he that taketh a city" (16:32). Though religious leaders tried to provoke Him to rash words, Jesus had mastery over His tongue. Peter wrote that no guile was found in His mouth (1 Peter 2:22). Inner strength results in swiftness to hear, slowness to speak, and delay in anger (James 1:19). "Self-control means controlling the tongue" (Prov. 13:3, TLB).

• Avarice. With the media screaming its commercials at us, luxuries can so easily become necessities. The easy payment, the need for status symbols, credit cards, gambling opportunities, all promote the spirit of avarice. Wanting something badly enough becomes idolatry.

Jesus warned, "Beware of covetousness" (Luke 12:15). Paul pointed out that "the love of money is the root of all evil (1 Tim. 6:10). The writer of Hebrews enjoined, "Keep your lives free from the love of money and be content with what you have" (13:5, NIV).

In our materialistic society we need self-control in the realm of possessions. This inner strength will help us to be giving instead of grasping, and thus cut the nerve of covetousness.

• Sloth. The writer of Proverbs condemned laziness. "I went by the field of the slothful . . . and, lo it was all grown over with thorns, and nettles had covered the face thereof, and the stone wall thereof was broken down. . . . Yet a little sleep, a little slumber, a little folding of the hands to sleep (24:30-31, 33).

The sluggard is told, "Go to the ant . . . consider her ways, and be wise," because she works hard in the summer to harvest food for the cold winter (6:6, 8). Inner strength will rouse us out of lethargy and make us diligent.

Summing up, the intemperate drinker or eater, the immoral, the spendthrift, the gossip, the youth with poor study habits, the lazy, the irregular church attender, the one who neglects his devotional time—all need self-discipline.

Act—Don't React

A preacher used to get upset when an approaching driver didn't dim his headlights. One night the preacher lost his cool and for two minutes let loose a barrage of abuse at the other driver who, of course, couldn't hear a word. Suddenly he got hold of himself, "Isn't it silly? Me a preacher and getting angry because a man refuses to dim his lights? That man has had control of me for two full minutes. Why should I let him rule my mood?"

We should not be reactors but actors. We should not let others control us, making us jump this way or that, depending on which way they pull us. Are we puppets at the ends of strings which they manipulate? Or are we people who hold our own strings? When a person says something nasty or vile to us, do we, like puppets, jump and revile? If so, we are reacting to their actions. They're getting our goat—and a rise out of us.

How unhappy is the perpetual reactor-puppet! His center of spiritual gravity is not fixed in himself where it should be, but in his environment. His spiritual status is always lifted or lowered by the spiritual climate around him, and he is always at the mercy of his surroundings. Criticism bothers him. Rebuke distresses him. Praise gives him a sense of well-being, but only temporarily. His surroundings govern him. He is a reactor-puppet instead of an actor-puppeteer. No calm of spirit will be his till he refuses to let others decide whether he will be rude or gracious, depressed or delighted.

In a book, *Pulling Your Own Strings* (Funk & Wagnall, New York, NY), Dr. Wayne W. Dyer includes a list of 100 typical situation-exercises to see how a reader scores on his "Victim-Profile." The trend of his answers will indicate whether the reader is a victim (reactor-puppet) or a nonvictim (actor-puppeteer).

For example, what would you do about a poorly served meal? If you tip the waiter the expected 15 percent, grumbling about the service as you leave, you would be a victim. If you left no tip and informed the management why you were dissatisfied, you would be a nonvictim.

Imagine that a fellow employee asks you to do a chore you don't wish to do, and are not required to do. If you go ahead and do it, feeling abused and bossed, you are a victim. But if you say no, without making any excuses, you are a nonvictim.

Let's see how this principle works in situations with spiritual implications.

• Response to God's laws. Daniel's three friends, ordered to bow down to Nebuchadnezzar's image, could have reasoned, "Everybody's doing it, and if we don't we'll be thrown into the fiery furnace." But they did not give in to these strong pressures but asserted their inner strength and refused to bow.

Virile Joseph, propositioned by Potiphar's wife, resolved to resist her allurements, though it meant running the risk of offending this lady of high position. He acted with the strength of his conviction, a puppeteer in charge of his conduct. S. Francis de Sales said, "We are not masters of our own *feeling,* but we are by God's grace masters of our *consent.*"

• Anger. When the herdsmen of Abraham and Lot fought with each other, Abraham could have angrily insisted on his rights, but he let Lot take over the well-watered area near Sodom.

When someone is out to get you, instead of seeking revenge, ask for the Spirit's strength to respond with kindness. On two occasions David could easily have taken King Saul's life, but David would not lift his hand against the Lord's anointed. Major-league baseball catcher Darrell Porter, after a bout with alcoholism, was sometimes needled by fans. He commented, "The only way they can hurt me is if I *let* them."

How easily parents can get mad at children who keep disobeying, even after repeated urgings or commands. In his film, "The Strong-Willed Child," James Dobson shows the futility of such angry response. He advises stating in advance what punishment will be meted out if a particular limit is overstepped, and then acting at the first disobedience. Firmly, and in full self-control, the parent should administer the penalty.

• Neurotic guilt. We need inner strength to absolve ourselves in situations involving unnecessary guilt. Almost always when someone passes away, loved ones berate themselves for not having done enough. "If only I hadn't left the room for those few minutes, maybe he wouldn't have died."

Perhaps you wanted to take a Cambodian refugee but couldn't. You need inner strength to assure yourself that several circumstances made it impossible. You rent a small apartment with no guest room. You work five days a week and you live alone. But you are giving several hours each week to tutoring a refugee in English.

Perhaps your child has rebelled against the Christian faith, and you need inner strength so as not to incriminate yourself. Realize that your child has his own free will. John White, Canadian psychiatrist, in his book, *The Fight,* says:

Different children will respond to the same disciplinary "causes" with a variety of "effects." The race is not to the parentally swift nor the battle to the child-rearing strong. The child chooses. He cooperates with the process or he sabotages it. The best parents in the world sometimes produce monsters; while the breakers of every child-rearing rule may produce a family of responsible, adjusted little angels. It happens all the time. . . . God is not a Celestial Programmer (InterVarsity, p. 113).

Parents need sufficient inner resources so as not to let parental happiness depend on successful outcome of child-rearing efforts.

• Esteem of others. The president of a company was walking down the hallway near his office when a stranger passed. He thought, "Does he know I'm the president?" So he called to the stranger, and in the ensuing conversation let him know who he was.

When we need to boast, or get attention, put up a bravado front, make noise, or act the big shot, it's a sign that we lack inner strength. Children from broken homes often misbehave to compensate for their feelings of inferiority.

If you have a strong inner confidence, you won't depend on the approval of others, nor will you let yourself be imprisoned by the expectations of others. Some people, whenever constructive criticism is given them, always jump on the defensive. But people with self-control can accept suggestions, listen to reproof, not take it personally, and even take some abuse and not be devastated.

• Adversity. No believer is exempt from trouble. Says Proverbs, "If thou faint in the day of adversity, thy strength is small" (24:10).

When we find ourselves in a trying position, we should immediately refuse to permit ourselves to be controlled by that situation. We should not be under but above the circumstances, acting as puppeteers, believing that God is going to use our situation for His glory. Paul, imprisoned in Rome, could have moaned about his severe limitations for witness and given up. But he mastered the situation, using it to advance the Gospel (Phil. 1:12). Many, like Onesimus, were won to Christ right in Paul's house-prison. Guards from the Praetorium couldn't escape Paul's message, and some of them became believers, right in Nero's palace. Paul also wrote several epistles from prison which are now part of our New Testament. Reaction to adversity can make us either better or bitter.

Job's inner strength was sufficient for his troubles. After several calamities, loss of property, health, children, and his wife's support, he exclaimed, " 'The Lord gave, and the Lord hath taken away; blessed be the name of the Lord.' In all this Job sinned not, nor charged God foolishly" (1:21-22).

Our Lord had perfect composure in the Upper Room, even knowing that in less than twenty-four hours He would be suffering utmost agony on the cross. Yet He said, "My peace I give unto you. . . . These things have I spoken unto you that My joy might remain in you, and that your joy might be full" (John 14:27; 15:11). The disciples should have been comforting Him, but it was He who comforted them, "Let not your heart be troubled" (14:27).

When adversity comes, the Spirit's presence gives us the strength to look to our God who is too wise to make a mistake, too kind to be cruel, who knows the end from the beginning, and who works all things out to His glory and our good.

Source of Inner Strength

A young lady claimed that she learned self-control by thinking how her late father would react in the same situation. Though such an example doubtless has value, the real source of the believer's inner strength is the Lord Himself.

In ancient times, nations trusted in other nations, horses, chariots, armies, or implements of war. In modern times, people turn to drugs, music, hobbies, amusements, and a host of other crutches. But none of these gives the needed strength.

Just as trees send their roots down into the earth to draw up the necessary water and minerals, so believers must draw upon the deep resources God places within them through faith in Christ. Paul said, "I am ready for anything through the strength of the One who lives within me" (Phil. 4:13, PH).

After the miraculous crossing of the Red Sea, the Israelites sang, "The Lord is my strength and song" (Ex. 15:2). David must have frequently strengthened himself in the Lord his God (1 Sam. 30:6). He wrote in the Psalms, "The Lord is the strength of my life" (27:1).

Nehemiah's inner resources enabled him to lead in the rebuilding of the walls of Jerusalem despite strong opposition.

Isaiah said the source of his strength was the everlasting God and Creator who never wearies nor faints. He added that those who wait for the Lord shall renew their strength (40:28-31).

Habakkuk, cut off from all outward possessions, exhorted his readers to be courageous and happy in God as their object of confidence (3:17-19).

Peter, emboldened by the Spirit, made an unanswerable defense before the Sanhedrin. When Paul was on trial and deserted by men, he had the presence of the Lord who stood with him and strengthened him.

F. B. Meyer said his life was revolutionized by a minister who instead of talking about giving up all for Christ spoke of "intaking from Christ." When unattentive children in church tempted him to impatience, he looked upward and said, "Thy patience, Lord!" Instantly, the Lord dropped patience into his heart. When a difficult situation tempted him to irritability, he would say, "Thy sweetness, Lord." And in a moment of weakness,

"Thy strength, Lord." Meyer said he learned the secret of intaking—taking in the Lord's strength to overcome the enemies of his soul.

Paul said, "Be strong in the Lord, and in the power of His might" (Eph. 6:10). He also prayed for believers, "Be strengthened with might by His Spirit in the inner man," through Christ dwelling in their hearts by faith (Eph. 3:16-17).

In November 1977 a flood devastated Toccoa Falls Bible College, killing thirty-nine, and causing $1.5 million damage. People at the Laboratory for Statistical and Policy Research at Boston College made a study of the survivors, and also of those who survived similar disasters in New York, Pennsylvania, Massachusetts, and Rhode Island. "On the whole," said the report, "the people at Toccoa Falls came out very well. They were in better mental health than those in communities who weren't hit so hard. Their very strong religious commitment gave them an understanding of what had happened. Because of Toccoa, we had to change our theory about psychological reaction to disaster to include cultural values." In other words, inner strength from their Christian faith enabled the survivors at Toccoa to fare better than others who suffered similar or lesser calamities.

To manage the wild within each of us, we need a tamer who can control our rebellious inner man. When we receive Christ, His Spirit comes within. As we let Him reign on the throne of our inner sanctums, His indwelling strength helps us live conquering lives.

Then, when we are masters of ourselves, we can be servants to others.

11
Enlarging Your Heart

In the early years of his writing, C. S. Lewis gave all his royalties to charity, informing his publisher where to send each check, so that Lewis never saw the money. When his books began to sell widely, his publisher wrote that a substantial sum (2003 pounds) was due him, and that he should think about income tax before assigning the money to charities. A friend figured how much tax Lewis owed on all past royalties. It was 2003 pounds—the same amount due him. From then on, royalties were sent to a charitable trustee, appointed by Lewis, who each year paid the tax due the government, and then on Lewis' instructions distributed the balance to people in need. It is estimated that Lewis gave away two thirds of his income and would have given more except for income taxes.

Lewis spent much energy answering letters by hand. He took considerable time writing what became *Letters to an American Lady,* filling the letters with down-to-earth advice, even though reportedly she was just "an old nag." Had he devoted the time spent in answering personal mail to writing books, it is estimated his literary output would have increased by 50 percent.

When an American correspondent, Joy Davidman, came to England with her two boys, the time limit ran out on her visa. Lewis married her so she and her boys could remain in England. Later, the marriage which had been born out of expediency blossomed into real love.

C. S. Lewis was a bighearted man. To have an enlarged heart physically may indicate cardiac problems, but to have a big heart spiritually signals a healthy condition. Paul told the Corinthians that his heart was enlarged toward them (2 Cor. 6:11). He made room in his heart unreservedly for them, despite wrongs done him.

The small-hearted person is rigid, narrow, critical, picayunish, and petty. Mean-minded church officials criticize their pastor (and wife) over minor, unimportant, and irrelevant matters. The big-spirited person is magnanimous, one who minimizes the faults of others, overlooks slights, delights when others succeed, and hurts when others have trouble.

Let's look at some of the actions you will take if you are becoming bighearted.

Overlook Offenses

Mrs. Jones is up the miff tree. She'll never darken the door of her church again. No real reason exists for her pique. Perhaps no one thanked her for paying an underprivileged child's way to a winter retreat. Or was it because her name was accidentally omitted from the list of those responsible for the Easter play costuming? She ought to pray, "From pettiness, dear Lord, deliver me."

Paul told the Corinthians they should be big enough to refrain from going to court with a Christian brother, even though it might mean suffering wrong and fraud. Such lawsuits made the church a laughingstock to the world (1 Cor. 6:1-7). It is man's "glory to pass over a transgression" (Prov. 19:11). Instead of bottling up resentment, it's far better to have a heart big enough to overlook an offense.

Forgive

Joseph's brothers were terrified when he revealed his identity to them. They expected vengeance, but he magnanimously forgave them. Later, when Jacob died and the brothers thought he would surely now get even, he again "comforted them, and spake kindly unto them" (Gen. 45:5; 50:21).

Corrie ten Boom told how disturbed she was to hear the mention of a man who had been an informer for the Gestapo. She could not sleep that night or pray properly. By the end of the week she had worked herself into such a sickness of body and spirit that she blurted out she would kill the informer were he to walk by. All this time Corrie was puzzled at her sister Betsie who had suffered as much but who seemed to carry no rage. "Betsie," Corrie hissed one dark night when she knew her tossing was keeping Betsie awake, "don't you feel anything against that informer?"

"Oh, yes, Corrie, terribly! I've felt for him ever since I knew— and I pray for him whenever his name comes into my mind. How dreadfully he must be suffering!"

Later that night Corrie was able to pray for the betrayer, and enjoy sleep for the first night in days. Saintly as Corrie was, many feel Betsie had an even bigger heart.

Return Good for Evil

In Chicago a few years ago a major newspaper had a fire that burned out its pressroom. Competitors could have gloated, "Great! That paper won't be printing for several days. We'll grab readers away from them." Instead, all other papers offered the use of their presses to the burned-out publisher, enabling him to stay in business without missing an issue.

When Paul was in prison at Rome, other preachers took advantage of his imprisonment and tried to promote their viewpoints through zealous preaching. But Paul responded with joy that Christ was being preached, even though with envious and contentious spirit.

A drunken man pounded loudly on the doors of a Salvation Army Corps center, asking for shoes. While the man continued to curse vehemently, the Salvation Army officer asked his size. With more curses he told his size. In the midst of further abuse, the officer ushered him to a seat and went to get some shoes. Returning with several pairs, the officer knelt in front of the drunken rascal, trying to fit him. Once the stranger spat in the officer's face, but he never answered, just kept on fitting him. When the officer found the right pair, he gave them to him, then ushered him to the door gently and kindly, and sweetly dismissed him.

Paul wrote, "See that none of you repays evil for evil, but aways seek to do good to one another" (1 Thes. 5:15, RSV). Instead of taking eye for eye and tooth for tooth, the believer is told to turn the other cheek, go the second mile, and love his enemies. Paul was confident that Philemon would show a large heart by not only forgiving his runaway slave, Onesimus, but by accepting him back as a Christian brother, and perhaps granting his freedom.

"Be ye kind one to another, tenderhearted, forgiving one another, even as God for Christ's sake hath forgiven you" (Eph. 4:32). How generous the forgiveness of Christ who when reviled, reviled not again, but kept saying, "Father, forgive them, for they know not what they do" (Luke 23:34).

Kierkegaard wrote of "heart-room," that spaciousness of heart that allows a loving family of five to live in a room that would seem cramped with one obnoxious person in it. Heart-room is what we need to love as unconditionally as Jesus did.

Do Not Show Off but Be Benevolent
If I sing my solos to show how superior I am to other singers, that's small-heartedness.

Felix Mendelssohn agreed to play with two other pianists in a three-piano piece. Just before they started, he discovered the other two had to concentrate on the score. Though he knew the music by heart, he placed some music on the rack, and asked a friend to turn the pages for him.

Delight When Others Are Honored
When the women sang, "Saul has slain his thousands, and David his ten thousands" (1 Sam. 18:7), Saul wasn't big enough to accept David's superiority, but tried to kill him from that day on. But Jonathan, rightful heir to the throne, had room enough in his heart for David, even if it meant David would reign in his place.

Do we appreciate it when a fellow worker is praised or given a job which we think we deserve? Not, do we seem outwardly sweet, but are we internally happy about it, praising God? Does a Christian Education director rejoice when the Sunday School superintendent is the one selected by the Board to attend the big Sunday School convention in Hawaii with all expenses paid?

When John Wesley's father, Samuel, was away from his Epworth church on a prolonged absence, his wife, Susannah, had a devotional time with her children on Sunday nights. A few neighbors asked to come, and soon the group grew from 30 to 200. Susannah read a sermon and prayed with the people who came. When her husband objected to these home meetings, Susannah defended herself, pointing out that more people now heard the Gospel. Mr. Wesley's assistant, Mr. Inman, also objected, partly due to the fact that more came at night than in the morning when he preached. The assistant's heart needed a little enlarging, so as not to take this evening success as a personal threat.

A bighearted person rejoices when a neighbor's child wins a scholarship, or another's business doubles, or a friend takes a trip around the world.

Act Unselfishly

Are we big enough, when our plan is rejected, not to become defensive or sow discord behind the scenes, but instead to throw our support behind the majority program?

A bighearted person takes in a wide range of prayer requests, not limiting himself to a group of workers from his own circle, but to a broad list of missionaries and organizations worldwide. It's not just the local church, but the church universal. One pastor forbade his youth musical group to ever minister in another church on Sunday or Wednesday. My thought is that while members should be primarily loyal to their own church, it wouldn't hurt for the group to minister elsewhere now and again.

At the National Religious Broadcasters closing banquet in Washington in 1983, a Billy Graham team member arrived at his assigned table and found all seats taken. A lady, without a right to do so, had turned up two extra seats, explaining she was saving them for her teenage son and his pal. The Graham worker had been specifically told to go to that table. When she remarked, "My son isn't a Christian, nor his pal. Neither has been in church for years," the gentleman, out of the bigness of his heart, volunteered to look elsewhere for a seat. The boys came a few minutes later, and heard a good message.

Overlook Pettiness

A twenty-five year old applied to be secretary in her church.

She was a faithful member, attending all regular meetings of the church. In addition, she was a very competent secretary. But the pastor, in a vendetta against the girl's parents, because they had left the church to attend a nearby house of worship, blocked her appointment to the secretarial spot.

Petty people harbor roots of bitterness which can spring up, cause trouble, and defile many (Heb. 12:15). Little-hearted people "bite and devour one another" and are "consumed one of another" (Gal. 5:15). One elderly lady was always bringing up what her daughter-in-law did to her forty years before.

A small person gets quickly impatient at the roommate who doesn't keep his half of the room spotlessly neat, or at the slowpoke driver who makes him miss the green light. When a Christian high school sent out a little bulletin each month, edited by the president, one man wrote, "I enjoy your bulletin. The first thing I do when it comes is to look for errors." Perhaps a Rochester, New York church had this type of smallness in mind when it carried this bulletin item, "We deliberately put some mistakes in here so you will have the satisfaction of finding them."

A little girl prayed, "Lord, make all the bad people good and all the good people nice."

Put the Best Light on Things

A couple was going to a counselor. During the course of the counseling, the counselor asked the wife to bring in a list of good things she saw in her husband, and also a list of the bad things. Next week she brought in one small sheet listing his good qualities, and a one-inch thick book of grievances in which she had been recording his bad points for over three years. A big heart does not keep such a record.

While at Ravensbruck concentration camp, Corrie and Betsie ten Boom found themselves in a room swarming with fleas.

When Betsie said, "Let's thank God for every single thing about this new barracks," Corrie just stared in amazement at her sister. The foul-aired, flea-ridden room received little supervision from the guards, enabling Betsie to read the Bible and witness to those around. One day Betsie exclaimed to Corrie, "I've found out why we have so much freedom in the big room. This afternoon there was an argument and when someone sent for the supervisor, she wouldn't come. Know why? She said, 'The place is crawling with fleas. You won't get me in there!' " A big heart can accept adverse circumstances, knowing that God has a reason for the situation, and that someday they will understand.

A big heart is not judgmental but gives others the benefit of the doubt. When someone parks in your designated space, perhaps he's a stranger who doesn't realize he has taken a private parking area, or maybe an ill person who needed a parking place quickly. Love isn't quick to condemn, but waits for an explanation before blowing off.

Love hides a multitude of sins (1 Peter 4:8). Instead of seeing how strongly we can place the blame, we cover the matter over. The lad whose mother asked how he had hurt his hand replied, "I scratched it on the cat." Love "beareth all things" (1 Cor. 13:7) is literally, "Love puts a roof on all things."

Spurgeon said, "Love stands in the presence of a fault with a finger on her lips." A big heart plays the game of Christian cancellation. When a critic says of a boy, "He does poorly in his schoolwork," the generous soul retorts, "but he studies hard, and seeks extra help from his teachers."

A group of university professors met regularly to consider recent acts of student misconduct. A professor insisted on a severe punishment for a student, commenting, "After all, God has given us eyes." One of his colleagues with a kinder nature replied, "Yes, and eyelids too!"

Even when forced to accept the ugly truth that a brother has committed a fraud, the big heart takes an optimistic view of the future. Just as God sees what we will be ultimately, so we should see others as they might be someday. The generous heart "hopeth all things" (1 Cor. 13:7).

Be Open to All Kinds

James instructs us that a shabby man who enters a church meeting is to be shown as good a seat as a rich visitor with a gold ring and fine clothes (2:1-4). The Old Testament repeatedly required kind treatment for the poor, the widow, the orphan, and the stranger. It takes a big heart to take in a refugee family.

A young man lived with a younger woman to whom he was not married, and had children by her. The man's mother, a devout Christian, was grief-stricken by his conduct, but gave her grandchildren great love. Even when her son suddenly died at forty, she continued her kindness to the children, giving them Christmas and birthday presents.

Christ received the immoral woman of Samaria. He also let a well-known sinner wipe His feet with her hair, even though this must have been somewhat of an embarrassment to Him.

The elder brother of the Prodigal Son needed expansion of heart to the size of his father's to welcome back his brother. Erring brothers are to be restored by spiritual brethren.

The Corinthian who had repented of his immorality was to be restored and tenderly comforted lest he "be overwhelmed by excessive sorrow" (1 Cor. 2:5-8). Corinthian hearts needed to be widened to accept all God's gifted servants: Cephas, Apollos, and Paul (1 Cor. 3:4-9).

Grand benevolence reaches out to the least, last, lowest, and lost.

Have a Wholesome Attitude

Back in the 1930s, young Dr. Martin Lloyd-Jones of England

confronted Dr. T. T. Shields, a pastor in Toronto, Canada, because of his strong attacks on theological liberals. Shields defended his mincemeat handling of the liberals by pointing out that when a patient has cancer, it's necessary to operate to save the patient's life. Lloyd-Jones retorted that a knife-happy surgeon is in danger of operating too quickly, always thinking in terms of surgery with rarely a thought of a second opinion.

Shields countered that when Peter defected from a position of grace by refusing to eat with Gentiles at Antioch, Paul may not have wished to oppose an older, honored apostle, but had to do it for the truth's sake. He asked Lloyd-Jones what he would say to that. Lloyd-Jones answered that the effect of Paul's rebuke to Peter was to win Peter to his position and make Peter call him, "Our brother, Paul." He then asked Shields if his attack on people led them to call him "Brother."

Shields admitted his contention did not have the same effect. At that point Lloyd-Jones made an appeal to Dr. Shields. He reminded him that he used to be known as the Canadian Spurgeon, gifted in intellect and preaching ability, but that in the 1920s he had suddenly changed to become negative and denunciatory. Lloyd-Jones urged him to drop his condemnatory preaching and return to his former positive presentation of the Gospel. It is said that Shields was moved deeply, but after discussing the matter with his board, was advised to forget Lloyd-Jone's advice.

A bighearted contender of the faith will necessarily have to warn against liberals, but should do it in the spirit of compassion and winsomeness.

Be Caring

So many Old Testament commands were given to provide care. Anyone who found his brother's, even his enemy's animal fallen or wandering was to bring it back to its owner, even taking care of it overnight, if necessary (Deut. 22:1-4; Ex. 23:4). Anyone building a new house was to construct a parapet around the flat roof to keep people from falling off the top. A small heart would say, "Why spend money on a safety feature?" But a big heart would not want to see anyone hurt (Deut. 22:8).

The bestseller, *The Chosen,* by Chaim Potok deals with two young men growing up in New York City in the 1940s, one a Reform Jew, the other the son of the head of a strict Hasidic synagogue. This Hasidic headmaster never speaks to his brilliant and athletic son except in religion classes, though he is fatherly to his other children. Only at the end of the story does the father explain this silent treatment, saying in effect, "God blessed me with an incredibly smart son. I found him at four years of age reading a horrible story of Jewish persecution, then with his photographic memory proudly repeating it, but without the slightest bit of remorse for the persons involved in the suffering. I cried to God, 'What have You done to me? I don't need a mind like this in my son. I need a son with a heart, soul, compassion, mercy, who can suffer pain—but not a mind without a soul. Better to have no son at all than to have a brilliant son with no heart.' Perhaps I was cruel in drawing away from him, but see—through my silence he has learned."

We need hearts that care as well as minds that know. A proverb says, "No one cares how much you know till he knows how much you care."

Be Generous

In the Old Testament economy, every seventh year an owner was supposed to release his slaves. As that year neared, an owner would be tempted to stingily shut his hand against his poor brother. But the law said rather that he was to open his hand to him, and "lend him sufficient for his need," and not have the base thought in his heart to withhold, because the year of release was approaching (Deut. 15:8-9).

When David and his followers were chasing those who had stolen their wives and possessions, 200 of the men became faint, so stayed behind to guard their possessions. When the wives and possessions were recovered and the enemy defeated, some of the more energetic soldiers didn't want to give any share of the spoil to those who didn't go to battle. But David in bigheartedness insisted that the 200 who stayed behind with the goods and protected them receive an equal allotment (1 Sam. 30:21-25).

"He that hath a bountiful eye shall be blessed (Prov. 22:9). The virtuous woman "stretcheth out her hand to the poor; yea, she reacheth forth her hands to the needy" (Prov. 31:20). Brotherly love will show hospitality to strangers, kindness to prisoners and the ill-treated, and share what it has (Heb. 13:1-3, 16). When a Canadian pastor finished a wedding ceremony, the groom, instead of giving him a fee, asked if he could borrow money to start them on their honeymoon. The pastor slipped him some cash.

A national paper told of a retired eighty-year-old sea captain who walks or bikes daily to a dump site two miles from his home in Horseshoe Bend, Florida to search for salvagable clothing, household goods, and appliances. Then he struggles to haul these cast-off goods back home where he cleans and repairs them to give to needy families. A strong man for his age, he manages to get stoves, dishwashers, even old refrigerators into his wheelbarrow and to push them down the road home. He launders and patches the clothes he finds. He puts in eighteen hours a day and lives off a small amount of Social Security. Says a local pastor, "Besides giving clothing and furniture to people who've been burned out or lost their jobs, he's painted all three churches in town free." The article began, "For bighearted Ephraim Clark, charity begins at the dump" (*National Enquirer* August 1983, p. 45).

Mr. Greatheart, a character in Bunyan's *Pilgrim's Progress,* is about to leave after giving some pilgrims a safe trip through the domain of wild animals. Christian says to him, "You have been so faithful and so loving to us, you have fought so stoutly for us, you have been so hearty in counseling of us, that I shall never forget your favor to us." Then Mercy says, "Oh, that we might have thy company to our journey's end! How can such poor women as we hold out in a way so full of troubles as this way is, without a friend and defender?" He was rightly named— Mr. Greatheart.

12
Upgrading
Your Devotion

In 1915 a company booked passage to England on the steam-ship *Lusitania* for one of its young employees. Soon after, the German Embassy issued a warning that the liner might be torpedoed, for it was during the early years of World War I. The owner wanted to call off the trip. "Don't worry," the youth replied, "I'm a strong swimmer. When I read about ships being sunk in the Atlantic, I began hardening myself by spending time every day in a tub of ice water. At first, I could stand only a few minutes, but this morning I stayed in the tub nearly two hours."

The owner laughed, for it sounded preposterous. But the youth sailed, and the *Lusitania* was torpedoed. The youth was rescued after nearly five hours in the chilly ocean, still in excellent condition.

Christians need to reach top spiritual condition through the discipline of a daily devotional exercise. To make the inner sanctum a holy place instead of a horror chamber, we must cultivate the practice of feeding the inner man. Isaiah said,

"They that wait upon the Lord shall renew their strength" (40:31). Victorious Christian living does not exist apart from a period of daily private devotions, the absence of which has been termed the number one reason for backsliding. The prac·tice goes by several names: manna in the morning, daily watch, trysting place, quiet time, daily devotions, personal devotion, individual worship, and the upper room.

Daily Nourishment

Some who like to have this period at the start of the day call it the morning watch. Abraham, Jacob, Moses, Gideon, Job, and David all met God early in the morning (Gen. 19:27; 28:18; Ex. 34:4; Jud. 6:38; Job 1:5; Ps. 5:3). The Lord Jesus "in the morning, rising up a great while before day . . . departed into a solitary place, and there prayed" (Mark 1:35).

Proponents of early devotions also point to historical leaders like Martin Luther who said, "If I fail to spend two hours in prayer each morning, the devil gets the victory through the day." John Wesley spent at least two hours daily in prayer, beginning at 4 A.M. (he went to bed early). Hudson Taylor often slept in the poorest of Chinese inns in a large room filled with travelers. In the morning, long before others awoke, he would light his candle and read the Bible and pray. He said that prayer in the morning was like tuning the orchestra before the start of the performance. Dr. J. Oswald Smith, missionary states·man, and founder of Peoples Church, Toronto, Canada, said, "For over sixty years now I have observed the morning watch. Because I meet God in the morning, I solve my problems before I come to them. Without the morning watch my work would be weak and helpless."

Going without breakfast is a poor habit; so is failure to have a spiritual breakfast. One Chinese Christian leader had a rule in his home, "No Bible—no breakfast." The need for early morning devotions is reflected in the radio commercial, "If the *New York Times* prepares you for everything, it's only logical to get it before everything."

However, some prefer their devotional period in the evening, like Isaac who "went out to meditate in the field at the even-tide" (Gen. 24:63). Others have more than one period per day, like Daniel who "kneeled upon his knees three times a day, and prayed, and gave thanks before his God" (Dan. 6:10).

Benefits

Because Mary sat at the feet of Jesus in the hour of sunshine, she was able to keep calm in the hour of sorrow, and to understand the death of Jesus more clearly than even the disciples, and thus anoint Him in advance. Spurgeon said, "If we don't come apart and rest awhile, we'll come apart."

Taking time for fellowship with the Lord makes us stronger spiritually, grants us self-disclosure, helps us evaluate our priorities and fix new strategies. Just as executives have revolutionized their lives by setting regular times to plan major activities for the future, so countless believers have dramatically altered their lives by providing time for spiritual inventory and projection.

Dr. Bill Bright, founder of Campus Crusade, says, "Your time alone with the Lord can influence every attitude and action." A man who had spoken harshly to his wife at break-fast realized during his first hour of work that he had neglected his quiet time that morning.

Daily devotion is like time-out in a football game when a team recoups its forces for the next play. It has also been likened to the winding of a watch, the tuning of an instrument, and the foundation of a building.

An article, "Why Pray for Missionaries?" ended by warning that unless a missionary enjoys spiritual victory in his own life he will eventually collapse, as many have, another scalp in the belt of the leering devil.

An editorial, dealing with how a young man could keep his faith in a liberal seminary, suggested that spiritual armor is fashioned out of the discipline of a day-to-day diet of God's Word plus the consciousness of a personal walk with Christ.

George Mueller came to see the danger of substituting action for meditation. To hurry to help in a public service without proper waiting on the Lord was to care more for quantity than quality of service. He said, "The primary business to which I ought to attend every day is not how much I might serve Him, but how I might have my inner man nourished." Oswald Chambers said that the biggest enemy to devotion to Christ is service to Christ. Especially is this true of a leader who can become very busy, neglect his inner life, and become easy prey to temptation.

Hidden in an African cornfield near a Nigerian city is an inconspicuous building enclosed by a fence about a block square. The building is one of eighteen tracking stations around the world, filled with electronic gadgets to keep track of astronauts as they fly through space—monitoring their pulse, blood pressure, temperature, and breathing. When the tracking station is in operation, no interference from the earth must be allowed, because the signal is so small. No cars are allowed within a half mile. The airport radar set several miles away is shut down. Similarly, we should try to remove every possible outside distraction in our devotional time so that we may track God's message for our hearts.

Phillips translates 2 Corinthians 4:16, "This is the reason that we never collapse. The outward man does indeed suffer wear and tear, but every day the inward man receives fresh strength."

Agenda for the Quiet Hour

A Navigator pamphlet, *Seven Minutes with God,* gives suggestions on "How to Plan a Daily Morning Watch." They call it a
"Daily 7-up," reasoning that five minutes may be too short, and
ten minutes too long at first.

The first thirty seconds are to be used for preparation of
heart by thanking God for the good sleep and the opportunities
of the new day, asking for cleansing, understanding of the
Scriptures, alertness of mind, and warmness of heart. Then
four minutes are to be devoted to Bible reading, allowing the
Word to strike some fire in your heart. Start with Mark and read
consecutively without a pause, perhaps twenty verses to a
chapter a day. Later move to John's Gospel, then to the rest
of the New Testament. The final two-and-one-half minutes are
to be spent in prayer. After a few days these seven minutes
could easily become seventeen, then twenty-seven, then even
more.

• Bible reading. The two main elements of a quiet time
involve the Bible and prayer. The Bible is spiritual food, likened
to both milk and meat. Jeremiah said, "Thy words were found,
and I did eat them" (15:16).

A man testified during an evangelistic crusade that he hoped
he would receive enough spiritual nourishment from the meetings to last him the rest of his life. Imagine hoping that a lavish
Sunday noon dinner would provide enough energy for the rest
of one's life, or even for a week. An army that didn't eat for a
few days would be too weak to fight. Does this explain why
some believers are not good soldiers of the Cross?

Nutritionists use the term "nutritional time bomb," referring
to deficiencies which remain undiscovered for years and then
suddenly manifest themselves in serious illness. The spiritually
undernourished person may discover, under adversity, that his
soul is too weak to weather the storm.

A Sunday sermon and a few scattered chapters during the week are insufficient. Read the Bible systematically. By reading five chapters on Sunday and three every day of the week, you will complete the Bible in a year. Also, try reading entire Bible books through at one sitting. Seventeen of the twenty-seven New Testament books have six chapters or less and can be read through in twenty minutes. Longer books can be read by units. When you receive a letter from a friend, you don't read one paragraph today, then another paragraph tomorrow, and so on. Treating the Bible as God's love letter, it is good to read the shorter books through at one sitting.

Billy Graham likes to read every day from Psalms for worship and from Proverbs for practical matters. By reading five psalms and one chapter from Proverbs daily, he covers these books every month.

One Navigator leader reads every thirtieth psalm. On the first day he reads Psalms 1, 31, 61, 91, 121. On the seventh day, it's Psalms 7, 37, 67, 97, 127, and so on.

• Bible study. The Bereans were commended because they "searched" the Scriptures daily (Acts 17:11). To avoid taking texts out of context to make pretexts—so often done by cults in building up their false systems—we should study to show ourselves approved unto God, rightly dividing the Word of truth (2 Tim. 2:15).

Essential study materials include various translations, a one-volume commentary, and a dictionary. Many people pursue their own course of Bible study, while perhaps as many others follow one of the many published courses available.

The purpose of Bible reading and study is not to become walking storehouses of biblical knowledge, but to be doers of the Word, not students only. The best version of the Bible is the translation into daily life. The Holy Bible is to issue in holy living.

A girl picked up a book of poems which seemed as dry as dust. Months later she fell in love with a man who was a poet and the author of the volume she had read. Now the poems came alive. They were the same old poems, but now she loved the author. When we come to know the Author of the Bible, that volume becomes alive, for we are devoted to the Author. It will be genuine devotional reading.

• Meditation is an integral part of the daily quiet time. (See chapter 4.)

• Prayer. After God has spoken to your heart through His Word, you will be ready to speak to Him in prayer. Your praying may well reflect your response to what was just read. Perhaps there's a command to be obeyed, a sin to be confessed, some guidance to be sought, some care to be cast on the Lord.

Your prayers should be specific, not just a vague "God bless so-and-so." How do you wish God to bless so-and-so? Intelligent requests demand research, such as careful reading of missionary prayer letters. If you have shopping lists, Christmas lists, why not a list of petitions you take before the throne of grace? Dr. Stephen Olford suggests seven lists, one for each day. Using alliteration, Monday is for missionaries, Tuesday for thanksgiving, Wednesday for (Christian) workers, Thursday for tasks, Friday for family, Saturday for saints (fellow believers who need to grow), and Sunday for sinners we want won to Christ.

Let's remember that we don't always have to ask for something. A father delights when a child just comes and sits on his lap without asking for anything. Through prayer God draws us into fellowship with Himself. That's devotion.

In 1535 Martin Luther wrote a long letter (forty printed pages) to his barber in answer to his question, "How do you pray?" Luther made the following points. Just as a barber must concentrate on the razor and not look around while he shaves, so prayer must possess the heart exclusively and completely if it is to be a good prayer. It is important to let prayer be the first matter in the morning and the last at night. We must not fool ourselves that some other job is more urgent, and so get sluggish, cold, and weary. Luther recommended using the Ten Commandments, the Lord's Prayer, and the Apostles Creed as prompters for thanksgiving, confession, duty, and action. A small portion of Scripture may spark the heart better than a long passage. He believed in having his quiet time with pen and paper in hand to capture God's nuggets and to later check up on himself. Such exercises, he maintained, warmed up his spiritual life.

For those who want to devote an hour to prayer regularly or on occasion, Dick Eastman has written a book, *The Hour That Changes the World.* He suggests breaking the hour into five-minute segments, though the duration may be longer or shorter according to the need of that period. The segments are: praise, waiting quietly, confession, praying in scriptural language, watching alertly, intercession for others, petition for self, thanksgiving, singing, meditation, listening for God's guidance, and praise, thus coming full circle.

• Other helps. Some like to use a book of daily devotions, like *Our Daily Bread* or *Streams in the Desert.* Among the personal possessions of Abraham Lincoln was a small book of daily readings called *The Believer's Daily Treasury,* which bore his signature in the flyleaf, and was well-worn with use.

Some like to keep a written journal, as Luther recommended. They use it as a device to encapsulate ideas otherwise lost. A Chinese proverb says, "The palest ink is stronger than the strongest memory." Later meditation on these captured truths may deepen devotion. Since 1940 I have kept a notebook to jot down thoughts that come in my devotions. Whenever I get the urge, I digress to follow some new thought till I exhaust its trail. How impoverished I would be without the hundreds upon hundreds of comments on biblical truth which have not only warmed my soul but have been passed on to others through classes, sermons, radio talks, articles, and books. Perhaps you'd like to try your own "mining in the morning."

Some are helped by fasting, which is far more than dieting. A voluntary abstinence from food as a spiritual exercise, a biblical practice not commanded but sanctified, this exercise reminds against gluttony, humbles or afflicts the soul, and helps one to concentrate on prayer.

• Retreats. Some advocate an annual retreat, involving a weekend of seclusion and silence in a Christian setting, away from ordinary activities, for complete occupation in spiritual exercise and meditation in godly matters.

Examples

During John Wesley's days at Oxford University he devised a strict discipline for his Holy Club. Its members spent an hour, morning and evening, in private prayer. At nine, twelve, and three o'clock they recited a collect. One hour each day was set apart for meditation. They fasted twice a week. They were certainly "Methodists" in their devotional practices.

Bill Bright says his devotional time begins every night before retiring when he spends the last moments of each day in the quiet of his heart with the Lord. He thanks Him for the bless-ings of the day, examines his heart and claims forgiveness for any displeasing attitudes or actions. Then he spends time read-ing the Word so that his last conscious thoughts are of God. Consequently, all night his subconscious dwells on the Lord, so that when he awakens in the morning, his first thoughts are likewise of Him. Again he acknowledges His Lordship, opens the Word for directions for the day, prays, and offers himself for service that day. For Bright, devotional life includes prayer, Bible study, and service. The inner strength from the quiet hour should result in outer service in the markets of life.

Charles Swindoll says,

> It's important to have a place, and usually the same place each time, but not in some "sacred" spot you can't reach in less than three hours. The place ought to be easily accessible and private—not on display so that others can watch me in prayer. I also include times of silence where I'm just with Him. Sometimes I'm on my knees; often I sit at my desk. But the focus is always on worship, praise, and adoration. (*Christianity Today,* 8 October 1982, pp. 54-56, © by *Christianity Today.* Used by permission.)

Psychiatrist John White tells in his book, *The Fight,* how as a medical student in England his life was changed by someone in an Inter-Varsity group giving him a card. On it was a quotation from the Gospels about Jesus spending a night in prayer. Underneath the text was this challenge, "God helping me, I resolve to spend at least twenty minutes daily in prayer to God." Below was a dotted line where he signed his name. Thirty years later White says that "a quiet song of joy is still flowing from my heart because of the ongoing revolution that little green card began."

Hindrances
The human heart by nature tends to shy away from this "closet duty." It's much easier to meet outside Christian responsibilities than to spend time with the Lord. Missionaries in Taiwan wrote that out on the field they had as much struggle as at home to maintain a daily time with Christ. The business of life makes it difficult to find time.

Failure to concentrate hinders the quiet time. To keep his mind from wandering, one man prays aloud. It's impossible to let your mind wander when you verbalize your thoughts out loud. Another man, who tended to fall asleep during his devotions, found it impossible to doze off if he walked back and forth in his "prayer closet."

Another hindrance is lack of discipline. You will have to be firm with yourself about a regular time each day, and this may mean getting up earlier. A Cambridge student, a missionary volunteer, found getting out of bed in time for a morning watch rather difficult. Determining to overcome his indolence, he invented a contraption which, when the alarm went off, pulled the covers off, exposing him to the cold morning air. When a young man asked George Mueller to pray that he might be able to rise each morning for a quiet time, the wise Mueller replied, "If you will get one leg out of bed, I'll ask the Lord to help get the other one out."

As suggested by Charles Swindoll, discipline requires a definite place as well as time. Jesus told the disciples to enter into their closets to pray. He meant they should get aside into a private, quiet place. For you it may mean a bedroom, a spare room, a corner of the living room, a literal closet, or the car in your garage. Jesus went up on a mountain to pray. Having a regular place says, "I'm trying to get apart from life's duties and distractions. Here I am. I do want to have a time of devotion."

After all is said and done, the quantity of time may not be as important as the act of spending time. Though some saints of old spent two or more hours in prayer daily, Spurgeon said he couldn't sustain a long period of prayer if his life depended on it. He explained, "It's like going to the bank with a check. I don't loaf around the premises after I already have my money."

Don't wait till all conditions are ideal. Start now, and learn by doing. A stranger in New York City called to a man walking near, "How do I get to Carnegie Hall?" Came the answer, "Practice, man, practice!" Plunge in with five minutes a day, and you'll likely be increasing it as the days go by.

A word of advice: Don't give yourself a guilt trip if you miss your quiet time now and again. (You miss meals occasionally.) Don't worry if you vary the length of your devotional period, sometimes short, sometimes long. And don't hesitate to change the order of the items, even omitting some. Avoid legalism and ritualism, and enjoy a balance of order and spontaneity.

Keep Thy Heart with All Diligence

In the hills above a European village an old man served as Keeper of the Springs. Patrolling the mountainside, he kept the springs pure by cleaning out deposits of silt, leaves, and decay, so the waters that came tumbling down were pure and cold. But one day lack of funds led the town council to abolish his job. Before long, the water was a green color, with scum on top. Leaves clogged the factory's machinery. Soon illness plagued the town. Up in arms, the townsfolk besieged the council to hire back the old Keeper of the Springs. Once more he made his rounds across the mountainside and once again, pure water flowed down to the village. People smiled. Sickness and odors subsided.

Paul prayed that he might "be strengthened with might by His Spirit in the inner man" (Eph. 3:16). We should keep our inner sanctum with all diligence, for out of it are the issues of life.